DREAMWE
T

by
Brad Halstead and Murray R. Summers

New Riders

201 West 103rd Street, Indianapolis, Indiana 46290
An Imprint of Pearson Education
Boston • Indianapolis • London • Munich • New York • San Francisco

Dreamweaver® MX Templates

Copyright © 2003 by New Riders Publishing

International Standard Book Number: 0-7357-1319-7

Library of Congress Catalog Card Number: 2002108274

Printed in the United States of America

First Printing: October 2002

06 05 04 03 02   7 6 5 4 3 2 1

Interpretation of the printing code: The rightmost double-digit number is the year of the book's printing; the rightmost single-digit number is the number of the book's printing. For example, the printing code 02-1 shows that the first printing of the book occurred in 2002.

Trademarks

Warning and Disclaimer

Publisher
David Dwyer

Associate Publisher
Stephanie Wall

Production Manager
Gina Kanouse

Managing Editor
Kristy Knoop

Acquisitions Editors
Linda Anne Bump
Todd Zellers

Senior Development Editor
Lisa Thibault

Senior Project Editor
Lori Lyons

Copy Editor
Kathy Murray

Senior Marketing Manager
Tammy Detrich

Publicity Manager
Susan Nixon

Manufacturing Coordinator
Jim Conway

Cover Designer
Aren Howell

Interior Designer/ Compositor
Gina Rexrode

Indexer
Cheryl Lenser

Contents at a Glance

Table of Contents

About the Authors

Brad Halstead (www.prettylady2.net) is a Computer Software Engineering Technologist by training, but deviated from that dream to join the Canadian Military as an Air Weapons Systems Technician. There he learned all about various computerized Aircraft weapons systems, as well as loading the munitions. Brad has dabbled in the Web in various capacities since 1989 and left the military to become a full-time computer technician. Brad tries to play an active roll in the support forums for Dreamweaver and Project Seven as time permits. He lives in London, Ontario, with his cherished partner Brenda and their 8-year-old daughter Megan, 13-year-old daughter Amanda, 12-year-old son Aaron, two Yorkshire Terriers (16-F and 12-M), and a cat (15-F).

Brad is HTML 4.01 Certified and has contributed a chapter to *Dreamweaver MX Magic* and made contributions to *Inside Dreamweaver MX* (both published by New Riders), in addition to being a technical editor for both publications.

Murray R. Summers is a Biochemist by training, but has spent the last 20 years working in the computer industry. In 1998, Murray started his own web site production company, Great Web Sights (www.great-web-sites.com). As a Team Macromedia Volunteer, he also participates in the sponsored newsgroups for Dreamweaver and other Macromedia products. He lives in rural Philadelphia with Suzanne, his lovely wife, their teenage daughter Carly, a golden retriever, an eskipoo, and some goldfish. As he sometimes gets up on the wrong side of the bed, you must be very nice to him on the newsgroups!

Murray is a Macromedia Certified Website Developer and Dreamweaver Developer, and has contributed chapters to *Dreamweaver 4 Magic* by Al Sparber (New Riders) and *Dreamweaver 4: The Missing Manual* by David Sawyer McFarland (O'Reilly), in addition to serving as technical editor on the latter publication. He has managed to embarrass himself several times as an invited speaker at TODCON (September/October/2001, Orlando) and will most likely do so again at TODCON II (September/2002, Chicago).

About the Technical Editors

Angela C. Buraglia After six years as an independent film makeup artist, Angela realized she wanted a career that would allow her to start a family and stay home with her husband and child. In an effort to give back to the Macromedia Dreamweaver newsgroup community that helped and encouraged her in her new career, she founded DreamweaverFAQ.com. Although she intended only to be a web developer, life's path has led her to become that and more. In addition to her contribution to this book, Angela is the lead technical editor for the *Dreamweaver MX Bible* (Wiley Publishing) and contributing author to *ColdFusion MX Web Application Construction Kit* (Macromedia Press). Currently, she is also a Team Macromedia Volunteer for Dreamweaver. Angela's future plans are to continue developing DreamweaverFAQ.com, to build and sell Dreamweaver extensions, to give presentations at conferences, and perhaps to become involved in new book projects. Be sure to look for her next accomplishment, *Dreamweaver MX Killer Tips*, written with Joseph Lowery, coming soon from New Riders. Long gone are the days of applying makeup; now Angela applies Behaviors and CSS to web sites—and most importantly—is home with her little boy.

Laurie Casolino first discovered the Internet in 1996, and it was love at first "site." The more she surfed, the more fascinated she became with the nuts and bolts of how web sites were created. She downloaded a freeware HTML editor and made her first home page. It wasn't pretty, but it was the beginning of a love affair with web design. Not happy with the lack of control she had over her page with this editor, Laurie started looking around for a good HTML editor. A friend recommended she try Dreamweaver. She downloaded the trial version of Dreamweaver 3 and immediately knew that this was what she had been looking for.

With two young children, Laurie wanted a career that met two requirements: 1) she had to feel passionate about it; and 2) she wanted to be able to work from home. Web design filled those requirements beautifully. In 2001, she started MJ Website Designs. Still passionate about Dreamweaver, she discovered the Macromedia newsgroups and the great bunch of volunteers who have taught her so much. Laurie started participating, soaking up knowledge, and before she knew it, she was helping others and giving back to the community that had given her so much.

Ryan Frank received his bachelor's degree from Purdue University, Indianapolis, in Computer Graphics Technology and is currently pursuing his graduate degree in Interactive Telecommunications at New York University's Tisch School of the Arts. He is currently employed at Brainstorm Design, Inc. Ryan has served as a technical editor on New Riders' titles such as *Inside Photoshop 6*, *Photoshop Effects Magic*, and *Photoshop 6 Artistry*. Ryan is an avid web and multimedia developer who has gained development experience using many technologies working for various graphic design firms.

Sean R. Nicholson is the Network Administrator and Web Developer for the Career Services Center at the University of Missouri - Kansas City. He and his development teams architect, develop, and manage foundation and backend execution for programs such as the CareerExec Employment Database (www.careerexec.com), UMKC Career Services Website (www.career.umkc.edu), UMKC's Virtual Career Fair (www.umkc.edu/virtualfair), and Kansas City United (www.kansas cityunited.com). Sean also does private contract work and consulting on database and web development with organizations and individuals.

Sean's technical publications include *Dreamweaver MX Magic* and *Inside UltraDev 4* (both published by New Riders), *Discover Excel 97* (Hungry Minds, Inc.), and *Teach Yourself Outlook 98 in 24 Hours* (Sams Publishing). He has also written several legal articles ranging in topics from Canadian water rights to the protection of historic artifacts lost at sea.

During his free time, Sean can be found traveling with his family, riding his motorcycle to biker events nationwide, or continuing the development of his site at www.unitedbikers.com, with the hopes of building one of the best biker communities on the web.

Dedication

This book is dedicated to all those who struggle with the concepts of web development, every day. Perhaps you will find a helping hand here.

Acknowledgments

We would like to thank New Riders Publishing for providing us with the opportunity to share our knowledge with you the reader; our Technical Editors (Angela Buraglia, Laurie Casolino, Ryan Frank, and Sean Nicholson), who kept us in line with queries and explanation where we were lacking; and our Editors, Linda Bump, Lisa Thibault, and Todd Zellers, for taking on the role of surrogate parents and tormentors. You guys are 'Da Bomb, Baby'!

We thank Sam Schillace for his knowledge and input with respect to Chapter 3. Sam assisted us with working through the Template Parameters, Passthrough Parameters, and Template Expressions sections by provision of content and explanation.

We would also like to thank Macromedia for such a powerful set of development tools. Without their hard work and engineering prowess, web development and Dreamweaver would not be what it is today. In addition, by generously providing us access to key engineering staff on the Dreamweaver MX development team (Heidi Bauer Williams, Donald Booth, Wanda Huang, and Sam Schillace), Macromedia has enabled many valuable insights and methods to be brought to light in this book.

Our appreciation goes to Amy Santos, Freelance Graphic Designer for Print or Web, of Allentown, PA, for providing her creative graphic skills to the look of the Hot Cool Toys site.

Finally, we would be remiss without mentioning the very generous support provided to Hot Cool Toys by Chicago Webs (www.chicagowebs.com), the industry's *premier* web hosting company, and Pat Stangler, who have donated the hosting space and account for this support site. Thanks Pat, Geoff, Tim, Jenny, and all the excellent staff at Chicago Webs.

Thank you one and all.

A Message from New Riders

As the reader of this book, you are our most important critic and commentator. We value your opinion and want to know what we're doing right, what we could do better, in what areas you'd like to see us publish, and any other words of wisdom you're willing to pass our way.

As the Editor on this book, I welcome your comments. You can fax, email, or write me directly to let me know what you did or didn't like about this book—as well as what we can do to make our books better. When you write, please be sure to include this book's title, ISBN, and author, as well as your name and phone or fax number. I will carefully review your comments and share them with the authors and editors who worked on the book.

Please note that I cannot help you with technical problems related to the topic of this book, and that due to the high volume of email I receive, I might not be able to reply to every message. Thanks.

Fax   317-581-4663

Email: linda.bump@newriders.com

Mail: Linda Bump
         New Riders Publishing
         201 West 103rd Street
         Indianapolis, IN 46290 USA

Visit Our Web Site: www.newriders.com

On our web site, you'll find information about our other books, the authors we partner with, book updates and file downloads, promotions, discussion boards for online interaction with other users and with technology experts, and a calendar of trade shows and other professional events with which we'll be involved. We hope to see you around.

Email Us from Our Web Site

Go to www.newriders.com and click on the Contact Us link if you...

- Have comments or questions about this book.

- Want to report errors that you have found in this book.

- Have a book proposal or are interested in writing for New Riders.

- Would like us to send you one of our author kits.

- Are an expert in a computer topic or technology and are interested in being a reviewer or technical editor.

- Want to find a distributor for our titles in your area.

- Are an educator/instructor who wants to preview New Riders books for classroom use. In the body/comments area, include your name, school, department, address, phone number, office days/hours, text currently in use, and enrollment in your department, along with your request for either desk/examination copies or additional information.

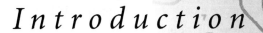

Introduction

Welcome to *Dreamweaver MX Templates*!

Even a simple website can contain hundreds of hyperlinks—to images, to other HTML pages within the site, to external CSS or JavaScript files, or to functions on external sites. It doesn't require an experienced webmaster to appreciate the tedium (and the potential for catastrophe) in manually updating each of those hyperlinks to reflect a new folder structure, a changed page name, or a new URL/domain name.

To accommodate such changes, Dreamweaver (DW) offers excellent link tracking capabilities in its Site Manager: Change a page name in the Site Manager, and all HTML links to that page will be updated to the new name automatically. That's a relief. But what if the reference to this page is part of a custom script, like the common JavaScript-based drop-down menu systems? Many times, such links are not visible to DW's site management features, meaning that a renamed or relocated page can cause the entire site's menu function to break.

How is it possible to manage even a modest site without having to "touch" every page to make these changes? DW's templates and library items can provide exactly these capabilities. Alternatively, server-side includes (SSIs) are very useful for such management challenges. Although the latter option may be the one you would choose for your application, and although this book will discuss (briefly) the use of server-side includes, the main thrust of subsequent content here will be to understand Dreamweaver MX (DMX) templates.

Other HTML authoring systems have implemented functions that have provided broadly similar capabilities as DW's templates, but it was Macromedia's understanding of the webmaster's needs that led to the parent-child relationship between templates and their associated dependent pages. This novel concept of templates was first introduced in DW2 (although DW1 already had library items) and has been with the Dreamweaver approach inclusive of this, the 5th version.

Dreamweaver MX (DMX) brings to the table a host of new and enhanced functionalities. Much has been improved or expanded with respect to templates, library items, and snippets, which happens to be the focus of this book. We have described in detail the utility of these functions in this book, and we hope that you will be much more comfortable and experimental in your application of these features should you choose to use their power for your projects. This introduction illuminates some of the considerations that we had to make during this book's preparation.

Reference and Project

As we explored the many cool things with respect to the subject matter, we decided to divide the book into two main sections.

Section I, "Reusable Page Elements," is the reference. We decided to include simple exercises with the reference section to reinforce what we are describing and focused on the reference aspect because the new template capabilities are so extensive. It is highly recommended that you read the entire book, or at the very least, Chapters 1 through 5 to gain the understanding needed to use templates, library items, and snippets efficiently with your workflow.

Section II, "The Project," is the project. Starting from a base template (a simple conversion from an .htm document), we take you through organizing the site, adding the various region types, and applying the knowledge gained in Chapter 3 about template parameters and expressions to build a complete website. We hope that you find this section as rewarding as the first.

By reading the book in its entirety, your creative juices will start to flow with ideas that may come from performing the various exercises in Section I and the project in Section II. Good luck in your exploration—we have had a blast learning from our writing of this manuscript.

Dreamweaver MX: Workspaces

Dreamweaver has different modes of operation now:

- Dreamweaver MX Workspace
- Dreamweaver MX-Homesite Workspace
- Dreamweaver 4 Workspace

The operation in each mode is similar, although each seems to have almost religious support in some camps. While definitely subjective, we have exercised our license as authors and opted to use Dreamweaver in Dreamweaver MX mode for the PC (mostly) because we find it to be the most versatile mode available to us for writing this book. While using this mode, if there is a difference in the methods used to access a menu item or a function of Dreamweaver, these have been pointed out for you in the text—but we have not exhaustively compared these operations among the different modes.

If you want to change your Dreamweaver mode to suit the screenshots and technology learned in this book, that is done from Edit > Preferences > General Category. When in this category, select the button labeled Change Workspace. In the Workspace Setup dialog, be sure that the only radio button checked is Dreamweaver MX Workspace. Depress the OK button to close the dialog, and press the OK button again to close the Preferences dialog.

There are other options that we have either enabled or disabled as well as extensions that we have installed, but none truly affect what we teach in this book.

Layout, Code, Design, and Split views

Dreamweaver has four view modes available to us: Layout, Code, Design, and Code/Design split.

Layout view has not found much support among the heavy Dreamweaver user community, primarily because its use shields the Dreamweaver operator from the reality of working with tables in HTML. We strongly recommend that you not use Layout view for your page design, and in fact, we don't even cover the menu options or the functionality of this operational mode in this book.

Code view and Design view each have certain menu items enabled or disabled, viewable or hidden. All this depends on open document type and functionality being accessed. Each has its caveats and Bravo Zulus (well dones!).

This book is written using Code/Design Split view so that the code being inserted into your page is viewable real-time, as well as the visual design impact of this code. Everyone operates Dreamweaver in different ways, though, and for the exercises in this book we strongly recommend Code/Design Split view so that you can follow along with optimal input from the page.

What (and Who) This Book Is For

Our main objective while writing this book was to be the authoritative reference for Dreamweaver MX Templates. If you've never used Dreamweaver before, or have used Dreamweaver but haven't used these features, you will find that this book will be a necessary reference that you can keep by your authoring station. In addition to its resource information, it provides a tutorial with a real-world example showing how to apply what you have read.

Even if you have used these features before in previous versions of Dreamweaver (only some were previously available), you will surely discover many new capabilities, just as we did in preparing this manuscript.

What's in This Book

Each of the book's eight chapters contains reference text, several hands-on exercises, as well as a real-work project that puts what's been learned to practical use. The chapters are grouped into two main sections:

Section I: Reusable Page Elements

In this section, the entire scope of templates (and their very useful offshoots of library items and snippets) will be examined in detail, with examples and mini-tutorials. Primary focus will be devoted to the extensive new capabilities that have been added to templates in DMX, and those capabilities will be illuminated while building a website for a fictitious company, Hot Cool Toys.

If you are already adequately familiar with DW and DMX Templates and would like to skip this section and head right into the practical part of this book, please jump to Section II, "The Project." The authors recommend that at the least, you skim Section I to discover the caveats and workarounds found during preparation of this manual.

Section II: The Project

In this section, you will build a fictitious company's website through a three-chapter project—basically a hands-on exercise in applying everything you've learned in Section I. Although Section I is not required reading, you are encouraged to read through it and work through the projects so that you are familiar with the menu items, locations, and associated dialogs.

Dynamic Code in DMX Templates

Although the concepts and methods described in this book will certainly work for static pages, they have not been fully tested when used in combination with server-side code. Even though this application of DMX templates is one of interest, it goes beyond the original thrust of this text.

How to Use This Book

Neither section is required: Some people learn by reading, others by working through exercises, and yet others learn best using both. It's really up to you how to proceed with the contents of this book.

- **Reading front to back.** This book has been written in such a way that no chapter is a requirement for the next, so feel free to read in the order that interests you, although care has been taken to organize it in such a manner that the logic unfolds systematically reading from front to back.

- **Doing the exercises or not.** The exercises are provided to give you practice with the topic at hand. You will benefit from performing the exercises, which are an encouraged part of this text's experience. There are times when you might not feel the need to perform the recommended exercise or you may want to come back later to perform it; so either way, the choice is yours as the exercises are built to reinforce what's been described in a textual manner. If you want to use the book as a reference only, you can find everything you're looking for in the text.

What to Take Away from This Book

We are so excited to be able to share details and our discoveries with you, and we hope that you will come away with knowledge and understanding that can immediately apply to your very own websites. When you close the covers of this book, you should have a greater understanding of how templates, library items, and snippets can work to your advantage when used appropriately and in concert with each other. Granted, templates aren't for every site, but they do have their advantages, applications, flexibility, and most certainly, power. However, as with anything else, you can't become a master by only reading a book! Go out yonder and practice what you've learned with your own sites, using this book as a reference as you need to. And above all else, have fun doing it!

Web Site Materials

Considerable thought was devoted to the issue of including a CD with this book, in the traditional manner. In the final analysis, it seemed more sensible to provide a support site with downloadable files simply because of the lead time required to produce a CD, many of which are out of date—or worse, obsolete by publication! In order to provide you with the most current version of the required files in the fastest possible manner, the authors will provide a support website, from which you can download all relevant files and errata.

At the support website (www.dreamweavermx-templates.com), you will find all files, images, errata, and other relevant material discussed in this book. Please visit this site to download the latest versions (which may have been changed since publication date) so that you can work with the most recent files.

The Working Files

There are two main files, compressed with a popular compression program for the PC (www.winzip.com). Each file is for a specific section in the book. You'll notice that the book is divided into two main sections. Section I is the reference/training section of the book, and Section II is more of a project-related section where there is more meat with respect to what you learned in Section I.

- **SectionI.zip**—All related files needed for the exercises in Section I of the book
- **HotCoolToys.zip**—All related files needed for the project in Section II of the book

There are also other files available for download—these will be clearly identified and relate directly to the book project in Section II and comprise the finished lessons. This will be accentuated with the actual sites being viewable online so that you can see the results in action on a live server.

All these files are downloadable from www.dreamweavermx-templates.com/register.cfm. Although registration is not required to download the necessary files, registration will provide its benefits to you by allowing us to communicate to you on subject material enhancements, errata for the book, and improved project files. Another reason that you should register is so that we can accumulate data on what groups of individuals are purchasing the book to provide to New Riders Publishing as statistical data. Once registered, you will be able to assign your own user ID and password to log onto the support site and get the latest and greatest!

After the book is published, there will be no further updates of these base source files. However, any changes that get incorporated into the download files will be available as a cumulative download by date of changes made (cumulative so that you don't have to download multiple file sets to get a complete set).

Downloadable Extension

Part of the download package available at www.dreamweavermx-templates.com is an extension entitled TemplateSnippets.mxp. This extension is a compilation of snippets that directly relate to template regions. Table I.1 details the snippets and their functions. Hard to track and remember what snippet is where, a PDF is available at our support website that has this table on it for printing purposes.

Table 1.1   The Extension Snippets

Group	Snippet Name	Snippet Description
Code Outside	Enable	Head—If a script is required before the opening HTML tag or after the closing HTML tag.
	Disable	Head—If no scripting is required before the opening HTML tag or after the closing HTML tag.
Expression	Expression Markup	Body—Template Expression (Long).
	Short Shown	Body—Template Expression (Short) Shown in Design view as @@ symbol.
	Short Hidden	Body—Template Expression (Short) Hidden in Design view.
	Passthrough Shown	Body—Template Expression (Passthrough) Shown.
	Passthrough Hidden	Body—Template Expression (Passthrough), hidden from Design view.
If	Single	Body/Wrap Selection—Single Template if statement, usually used with Optional Regions.
	M_Block text	Body—Inserts a Conditional MultipleIf code block with Text displayed when condition is matched.
	M_Block Comments	Body—Inserts a Conditional MultipleIf code block with comments for editing when condition is matched.
	M_Block Parameters Shown	Body—Inserts a Conditional MultipleIf code block with parameters displayed when condition is matched.
	M_Block Parameters Hidden	Body—Inserts a Conditional MultipleIf code block with hidden blank parameters when condition is matched.
	M_Line Text	Body—Inserts a Conditional MultipleIf code statement block with Text displayed when condition is matched. For use inside a MultipleIf conditional Block.
	M_Line Comments	Body—Inserts a Conditional MultipleIf code statement block with comments for editing when condition is matched. For use inside a MultipleIf conditional Block.
	M_Line Parameters Shown	Body—Inserts a Conditional MultipleIf code statement with Parameters displayed when condition is matched. For use inside a MultipleIf conditional Block.

Group	Snippet Name	Snippet Description
	M_Line Parameters Hidden	Body—Inserts a Conditional MultipleIf code statement with hidden blank parameters when condition is matched. For use inside a MultipleIf conditional Block.
Parameters	Boolean (true|false)	Head—Boolean Template Parameter.
	Color	Head—Color Template Parameter.
	Number	Head—Number Template Parameter.
	Text	Head—Text Template Parameter.
	URL	Head—URL Template Parameter.
Region Locks	Hidden	Region Lock—Prevents passthrough to nested templates when added to the nested template region and hides the @@ symbol from Design view.
	Shown	Region Lock—Prevents passthrough to nested templates when added to the nested template region and displays the @@ symbol in Design view.

Getting Help

Although the Dreamweaver F1 help files are in error in several locations, it is a valuable resource that you should peruse prior to posting tech support requests. Also, please explore the Macromedia Technotes, located at `http://www.macromedia.com/support/dreamweaver/technotes.html`. They also provide a wealth of information pertaining to all aspects and versions of Dreamweaver.

Enjoy the book!

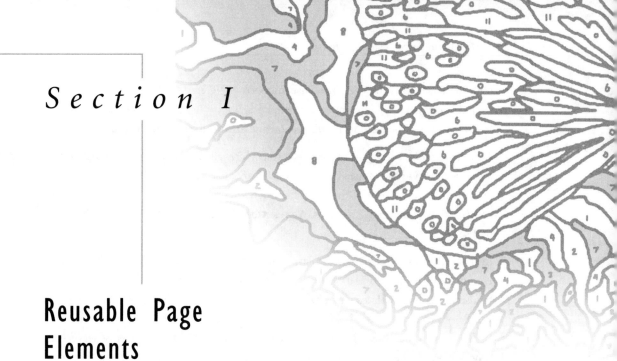

Section I

Reusable Page Elements

Before we actually apply hammer to nail

in creating the web site for Hot Cool Toys

(the focus of Section II, "The Project"), it's

important to make sure that you clearly

understand all terms and usages because this book often refers to specific properties of the "reusable elements" of Dreamweaver: templates, library items, and snippets. Please feel free to take what you need from this section and arm yourself for the coming project!

The files you need to complete this project are all available on the support site, www.dreamweavermx-templates.com/register.cfm, including PNG graphics and template files. You also will find other files there that represent intermediate steps in the construction of the template pages. We refer to these intermediate files throughout this first section of the book.

In this section, we will pay particular attention to the new template capabilities delivered in DMX. Although you could focus some of the same control on your site's pages by using DW4's templates creatively, there are many features in DMX that you would simply not be able to duplicate in previous versions of DW or Dreamweaver UltraDev. In fact, using the advanced control that DMX affords can put the power of server-side processing into the hands of design-time developers without requiring that they learn ASP, JSP, CF, PHP, and so on, or that they struggle with the (sometimes) arcane problem of connecting with a local web server. Much of the same decision-making and content-managing functionality that was available in DW is also present in DMX, and this is its greatest strength.

At the same time developers are liberated from needing to be fluent in the more complex server scripting methods, they also are relieved of the requirement to find an appropriately configured host. In other words, to use ASP in your pages you must be hosted on an ASP-capable server, whereas using the design-time processing in DMX imposes no such hosting restrictions.

Defining the Site

The exercises in this section are cumulative, which means that each builds on the same site definition and file set. Accordingly, please configure your Dreamweaver MX Site Definition as detailed here:

1. Download the file named SectionI.zip from www.dreamweavermx-templates.com/register.cfm.

2. After the file is downloaded, extract the zip file to a folder of your choosing. (You can put this folder anywhere on your hard drive—just be sure to remember its name and location!) Make sure the extraction retains folder information so that all the links work properly. You can use one of many popular archiving utilities, such as WinZip or StuffIt, to extract the file archive.

3. Name the new folder you created **DMXSI_Templates**. This will become the root folder of your project site.

4. Start Dreamweaver and configure a new local site as follows:

   - Select Site > New Site.

   - Click the Advanced tab and complete the fields as follows:

     Site Name: DMXSI_Templates

     Local Root Folder: Browse to and select the DMXSI_Templates folder you created to hold the extracted files. On the PC, this might be C:\DMXSI_Templates\ and on the Mac this might be OSX_Drive:Library:Sites:DMXSI_Templates.

     Default Images Folder: DMXSI_Templates\images\ (or DMXSI_Templates:images:)

   - Leave the remainder of the settings at their defaults (see Figure SI1).

   - Click OK to save the site definition and close the Site Definition dialog box.

Figure SI.I   The completed site definition.

5. Ensure that the site named DMXSI_Templates is selected in the Site panel. If there are no files or folders showing in the local site view, click the plus (+) sign beside the site name to expand the site files.

Proceed with the remaining steps of the exercises in the chapters from here. ∎

Chapter 1

The Snippets panel.

Snippets

With the templates and library items in Dreamweaver MX, is there really room for another type of "canned" code? There certainly is, and this chapter is a good place to learn how snippets can fit into that picture.

In this chapter, you learn what Dreamweaver MX (DMX) snippets are and discover how to do the following things:

- Access the Snippets panel.

- Insert, create, edit, and delete snippets.

- Manage snippets.

- Share snippets.

- Build snippet extensions.

In this chapter, you also learn about third-party extensions that relate to snippets.

Snippets Explored

From a single ASCII character to an entire page of HTML, JavaScript, and server-side code, a snippet can be anything you can imagine, subject to the limitation of being placed on an HTML page. A snippet can be code and only code, and it can reference images, library items, or Flash files; but it cannot store them directly, which means that a snippet cannot be an image or a library item.

You can use snippets to wrap currently selected code or to insert a block of code at the current cursor position in either Design view or Code view. You can preview snippets in the Snippets panel using Code view or Design view. (Experiment with your custom and default snippets to determine the best insertion and preview methods for you.)

 Note

> Inserting a snippet in Design view affects only the body region. You must use Code view to insert snippets that affect the head region of the document or that need to be inserted above or below the HTML tags of the document.

Snippets have been around in other Macromedia products for a few versions now: Homesite, ColdFusion Studio, and JRun Studio. These applications could all share snippets with ease by using a shared snippets folder configurable through the programs' Preferences, Configuration, and/or Options commands. Snippets are brand new to Dreamweaver MX and are no longer sharable with these other applications. (The exception is Massimo Foti's Classic Snippets extension, covered later in this chapter, which was available for Dreamweaver/UltraDev version 4.x). The snippets are no longer sharable because they are now held in a single XML file and have a new file extension of .csn. This .csn file stores all snippet information, including the start and end code if you have wrapped mode selected. The other applications use .hss for the snippet start code and .hse for the snippet end code.

Template regions and library items are explored extensively in Chapters 3 and 4, respectively, so you will become familiar with their power and functionality. Snippets bring other simpler things to the table while sacrificing some functionality that you may be accustomed to with library items.

You can insert a snippet on a page as many times as you want. You can modify each of this page's identical snippet instances to be unique, even when the snippets are used multiple times on the same page. This is unlike a single library item, which always produces the same code when it is used multiple times on the same page. If you change the actual snippet in the Snippets panel, the changes do not propagate to any document in which the snippet has already been used—in other words, no relationship exists between the snippet and the snippet instance (no parent/child effect). This means that any snippet you update must also be updated in the pages on which they were used.

> **Note**
>
> Unlike library items and templates, snippets are simply code fragments inserted in your page, with no DMX-related management. DMX is not configured to create, identify, or parse (check for) snippet-related comments. Because there is no way to identify a snippet once it is inserted in your page, there is no way to link any given snippet instance back to its parent code.

If you use a snippet in a library item or a template, any changes you make to the code *in these items* will propagate through the pages as expected.

> **Note**
>
> Also unlike templates and library items, snippets are not listed or displayed as a category of the Assets panel.

Perhaps the most wonderful thing about snippets is that they are globally available and not site-specific tools. This means that any snippet is available in any site on your computer, at any time!

Accessing the Snippets Panel

Like many items in DMX, there is more than one way to access the Snippets panel interface:

- Use the shortcut key combination of Shift+F9.

- Select the Code panel group expansion icon (see Figure 1.1) and click the
  Snippets panel tab. Your panel group may be different if you placed the Snippets
  panel in another group. The method outlined assumes the default panel configuration obtained when DMX is installed.

Figure 1.1   Selecting the Code Group expansion button.

- Use the Window > Snippets menu item (see Figure 1.2).

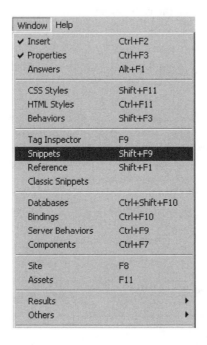

Figure 1.2   Selecting the Snippets panel using the Window menu item.

The Snippets Panel Interface

The Snippets panel (see Figure 1.3) is used to create, edit, delete, preview, manage, and
insert your snippets. The Snippets panel interface is straightforward, but this section
describes each item for you and provides some helpful tips.

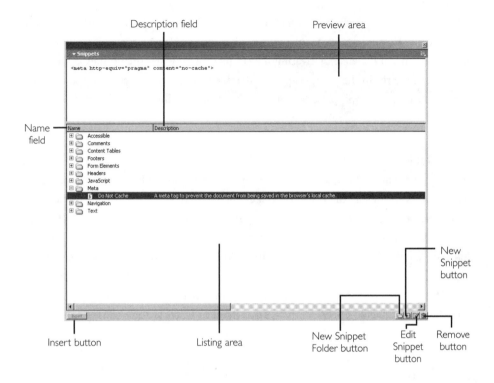

Figure 1.3   The Snippets panel ungrouped and expanded.

Preview Area

What you see in the Preview area depends on the snippet preview setting (configured at time of snippet creation or when the snippet is edited), so you may see either code or the actual visual design displayed here. The preview area displays as Code view or Design view and is used as a visual representation of the selected snippet. This field is blank if no snippet is currently selected.

> **Note**
>
> When creating or using snippets that contain template expressions (for example, @@(expression)@@), the preview pane of the Snippets panel does not display the expression as shown in Figure 1.3. For more information on template expressions, please see Chapter 3, "All About Templates and Regions."

Listing Area

The Listing area lists the recognized snippet folders, subfolders, and snippets and is organized in two columns (Name Field and Description Field). Clicking the right mouse button in this area selects the snippet at the current pointer location and populates a context menu that gives you the following menu options: New Snippet, New Folder, Edit, Insert, Rename, and Delete. Activating the context menu when the pointer is located in a null area (an area in the Snippets panel interface listing area that is not populated by a folder, sub-folder, or snippet/description) also deselects any currently selected folder, subfolder, or snippet.

Name Field

The Name field in the Listing area is the column used for snippet folder names and snippet names. You can sort the column by clicking the Name column header. You also can use the Name column header to deselect any selected folder, subfolder, or snippet so that you can create root level snippets and snippet folders. Be descriptive here; you will find that you can misplace your snippet due to the tree structure of the snippets listing. You can rename a snippet folder, subfolder, or snippet without actually editing the whole snippet using two methods: select the desired name, pause, and then select it again (the name becomes editable); or select the desired item, right-click, and choose Rename from the context menu.

Description Field

The Description column in the Listing area is the column used to display the snippet description as defined at snippet creation or during a snippet edit. The Description column has sort capability and can also be used to deselect any selected folder, subfolder, or snippet. Be descriptive here also; it will help your fellow developers when they use your custom snippets. Note that depending on your panel sizing, you may need to scroll horizontally to see the Description field in the Panel dialog. You also can adjust the spacing between the Name and Description columns headers by using the scrollbar that is located between the column headers.

Insert Button

The Insert button is disabled when no document is open, when the document view does not match the requirements specified at the time you created the snippet, or when no snippet is selected. Alternatively, you can use drag and drop to drag the selected snippet to your open document and release the mouse button to insert the snippet; or you can double-click the selected snippet to insert it at the current cursor location.

New Snippet Folder Button

The New Snippet Folder button is always active and is used to create a new untitled snippet folder anywhere in the snippet tree.

New Snippet Button

The New Snippet button is always active. When you click it, the Snippet dialog opens so that you can create a new snippet. The new snippet is inserted in the currently selected folder, and if there is no folder selected, the snippet is created at the snippet panel root.

Edit Snippet Button

The Edit Snippet button is disabled unless a snippet is selected. When you select a snippet and click the button, the Snippet dialog opens, showing the details of the currently selected snippet. If you want only to edit the folder, subfolder, or snippet name, select it, pause for a second, and then select it again. The Name field becomes editable. Press Enter or select another snippet to activate the changes. You also can right-click the snippet name and choose Rename from the context menu. If there is an illegal character in the name, you receive a warning dialog and the name reverts to its last saved state.

Remove Button

The Remove button is always active, but it does not do anything if no folder, subfolder, or snippet is selected. Alternatively, you can use the Delete or Backspace key to delete folders, subfolders, or snippets.

Warning

You can delete a whole tree if you haven't selected the snippet properly, and there is no Undo feature available to the Snippets panel. Once the selection is gone, it is gone! The only way to restore the default installed snippets is to reinstall DMX!

Using Snippets

Now that you know what a snippet is and how the Snippets panel interface works, it's time to find out how to manipulate these snippets of code by learning to insert, edit, create, delete, and manage snippets using the various snippet-related user interfaces.

Note

Snippet sharing and extension building are not handled through Dreamweaver user interfaces. These capabilities will be explored separately in this chapter.

Insert Snippets

You can use four methods to insert a snippet into your currently active document:

- Select the desired snippet. Using drag and drop, drag the snippet from the Snippet panel list area onto the desired target area of your page in Code or Design view, and drop it there.

- Position your cursor at the desired insertion point of your currently active document. Select the desired snippet in the Snippet panel listing area, and then click the Snippets panel Insert button (refer to Figure 1.3).

- Position your cursor at the point you want to insert the snippet in the current document. Right-click the desired snippet to bring up the context menu and select Insert.

- Position your cursor at the point you want to insert the snippet in the current document. Double-click the desired snippet and it is inserted in your document at the previously selected position.

Create a New Snippet

You can create a new snippet three ways:

- In the Snippets panel, select the New Snippet button (refer to Figure 1.3).

- Right-click the Snippet panel listing area to display the context menu and then select New Snippet.

- Select text or code in Design or Code view, right-click to bring up the context menu, and select Create New Snippet.

 Note

The third method opens the Snippet dialog, with the previously selected code already positioned in the Insert Before field.

The Snippet Dialog

You use the Snippet dialog (shown in Figures 1.4 and 1.5) to create and edit snippets.

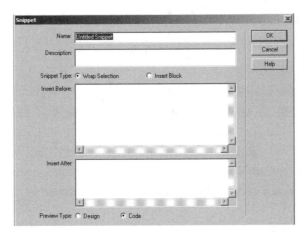

Figure 1.4   The Snippet dialog (Wrap mode).

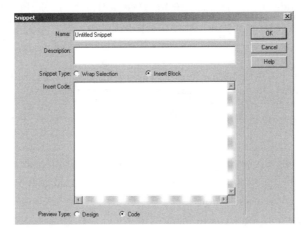

Figure 1.5   The Snippet dialog (Block mode).

Name

The Name field is where you name your snippet. Use something descriptive that you and your coworkers will recognize, and observe normal operating system-specific naming conventions. When you are creating a new snippet, the Name field contains Untitled Snippet until you name it.

Description

The Description field (optional) is where you can provide more information about the snippet. This area is a great place to tell others where the snippet should be placed (head or body) and let people know whether the snippet wraps other content or inserts as a block.

Snippet Type—Wrap Selection

When you select the Snippet Type—Wrap Selection option, the Insert Before and Insert After fields are visible, and the Insert Code field is hidden from view. Enabled, this option wraps the selected content in Code or Design view, placing the Insert Before code at the front of the selection and the Insert After code at the end of the selection. If you don't make a selection in Code or Design views, both code segments get inserted together. When you are creating a new snippet, this snippet type is selected by default.

Snippet Type—Insert Block

When you select the Snippet Type—Insert Block option, the Insert Before and Insert After fields are hidden from view, but the Insert Code field is visible. Enabled, this option inserts the snippet code at the current cursor position in either Design or Code views.

Warning

If you have content selected when you try to insert this snippet type, the selected content is overwritten with the snippet code, which can result in data loss.

Insert Before

The Insert Before field is dependent on the Snippet Type—Wrap Selection option. Code you enter in this field gets inserted at the front of your selected code in Design or Code view. If you have made no selection in Code or Design view, the content gets inserted at the current cursor position (refer to Figure 1.4).

Insert After

The Insert After field is dependent on the Snippet Type—Wrap Selection option. Code you enter in this field is inserted at the end of any selected code in Design or Code view. If there is no selection in Code or Design view, the content is inserted at the current cursor position after the code from the Insert Before field (refer to Figure 1.4).

Insert Code

The Insert Code field is dependent on the Snippet Type—Insert Block option. Code you enter in this field gets inserted at the current cursor position in Code or Design view (refer to Figure 1.5).

Preview Type—Design

When the Preview Type—Design option is selected, the Preview area of Figure 1.3 is populated with the snippet rendered the same as the Design view of Dreamweaver. The help documents say this field is optional, but in our experience, either it or Preview Type—Code must be selected, because the two options are a paired radio button set.

Preview Type—Code

When this option is selected, the Preview area of Figure 1.3 is populated with the snippet rendered the same as the Code view of Dreamweaver (you see the actual code). Although the F1 help documentation says that this field is optional, our experience using this dialog dictates that Preview Type – Design or Preview Type – Code must be selected. When you are creating a new snippet, this Preview Type is selected as default.

Edit Snippets

You can edit a snippet two ways:

- Select the desired snippet and click the Edit Snippet button in the Snippets panel.
- Select the desired snippet and right-click (or Ctrl+click in Mac) the Snippets panel; then choose Edit from the context menu.

After you have opened the Snippet dialog, it will be populated with the snippet data and look similar to Figure 1.4 or 1.5, depending on what your selections were when you originally created the snippet.

Delete Snippets

You can delete a snippet three ways:

- Select the snippet in the Snippets panel and click the Remove button (trash bin icon) in the lower-right corner of the Snippets panel (refer to Figure 1.3).
- Select the snippet you want to delete, press the right mouse button (or press Ctrl+click), and choose Delete from the context menu.
- Select the snippet and press the Delete or Backspace key.

Warning

Extreme caution should be exercised when deleting snippets using the Snippets panel. Should you inadvertently select and delete a snippet tree, the only way to recover it is to reinstall Dreamweaver MX.

Create a New Folder

To create a new snippet folder, deselect all snippet categories by clicking the name label at the top of the user interface, and then click the New Snippet Folder button (refer to Figure 1.3). A new untitled folder is created and you can change the name to whatever you like. This is a root level snippet folder.

You can create subfolders the same way, except that instead of clicking the name label to clear any selected folders or snippets, select your desired snippet folder "root" and then click the New Snippet Folder button.

There are some limitations for folder naming forced by the operating system, and these must be observed. If you use an illegal character or too many characters, Dreamweaver reports the error to you and allows you to re-create the folder or snippet.

As with other options, the New Snippet Folder is available from the Snippets panel context menu. The rules outlined previously apply.

Manage Snippets

The most difficult thing to do with snippets is manage them. To move a folder or subfolder into another folder, use drag and drop. The same applies for moving snippets around: Select the snippet, drag it to the desired new folder, and drop it. It's that simple.

The difficult part is getting yourself into a naming convention routine that makes sense to you and hopefully your co-workers. Naming folders, subfolders, and snippets appropriately is paramount to your mental health, as well as to your ability to easily locate your snippets later. Take advantage of the Description field as well, and you are sure to become a happy person!

Exercise 1.1:   Managing Snippets

Now that you know all the theory behind the various functions of the Snippets panel, you can put some of that theory to practical use in Exercise 1.1. In this exercise, you put all that you have learned about snippets into practical use through generalized examples. To completely understand snippets, you are encouraged to explore variations of this exercise on your own.

1. Make sure that you have the required site defined in DMX and that Dreamweaver is running. (If necessary, see the instructions provided in the section entitled "Defining the Site" in Section I, or start Dreamweaver if your site is already defined.)

2. Open the Code panel group and click the Snippets panel tab. Notice that the Accessible folder is highlighted but inactive. Click the Name column header at the top of the interface to deselect the folder. Notice that the highlighted folder becomes deselected and the sort order is reversed. Click the Name column header again. The same deselection and sort methods can be applied by clicking the Description column header.

3. Click the New Snippet Folder button and type **DWT** as the folder name. Press Enter.

4. Create another new snippet folder below the root using the context menu. Right-click (or press Ctrl+click) in the Listing area below the DWT folder you just created and select New Folder from the context menu (see Figure 1.6).

Warning

If you do not position the pointer properly, you will inadvertently select a snippet folder and insert this new folder as a subfolder.

5. Type **DWT_Delete** as the New Snippet Folder name and press Enter (see Figure 1.7).

6. Select the snippet folder named DWT and click the New Snippet icon, filling in the Snippet dialog with the following information (as seen in Figure 1.8):

   - **Name**: My Copyright

   - **Description**: Block—Inserts My Copyright notice (2002) wrapped in paragraph tags specified with copyr CSS class. Don't forget to define the copyr class.

   - **Snippet Type**: Insert Block

   - **Insert Code**: `<p class="copyr">&copy; 2002, Your name here._All rights reserved.</p>`

   - **Preview Type**: Design

7. Click OK, and the newly created snippet should appear in the DWT folder (see Figure 1.9).

Figure 1.6
The Snippets panel context menu.

Figure 1.7
The Snippets panel displayed with the two new snippet folders created in steps 3 and 4.

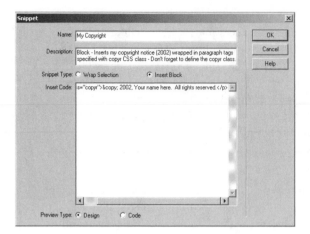

Figure 1.8   The completed Snippet dialog for the My Copyright snippet.

Notice that you used *Block* as the first word in the Description field. This tells you at a glance which insert mode the snippet uses. Also note that the HTML is rendered in the preview area because you chose Design as the Preview Type.

Warning

Snippets are not validated at time of creation. It is best to use your snippet on a page, check validation, and adjust the snippet until it passes validation. There is also no error checking in a snippet—if you use dynamic code in a snippet, it will not be checked for errors until it is used on a page.

Figure 1.9
The Snippets panel with the My Copyright snippet selected.

8. Create another new snippet in the DWT folder, using the context menu. Right-click (press Ctrl+click) in the Listing area below the last snippet folder. Select New Snippet from the context menu and fill in the Snippet dialog with the following information (as seen in Figure 1.10):

- **Name:** Paragraph with Copyright
- **Description:** (W)—Inserts paragraph tags with copyr class assigned. Remember to define the copyr class!
- **Snippet Type:** Wrap Selection
- **Insert Before:** `<p class="copyr">`
- **Insert After:** `</p>`
- **Preview Type:** Code

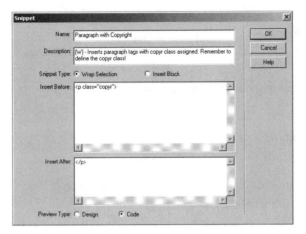

Figure 1.10   The completed Snippet dialog for the Paragraph with Copyright snippet.

9. Click the OK button and you should see your newly created snippet appear in the DWT folder.

   You used *(W)* as the first word in the Description field to
   show you quickly which mode the snippet uses to insert—
   in this case, Wrap. You now know two ways to provide
   yourself and users of your snippets with a visual guide of
   how the snippet inserts on the page.

Tip

Deciding on the best naming techniques is completely up to you
and your needs. Examples of naming conventions might be **Block-
Head** for head region block mode or **WB** for Wrap Body region
selected code.

10. Select the Paragraph with Copyright snippet you created
and drag and drop it onto the DWT_Delete snippet folder.
Notice that the folder automatically expands to show the
snippet, but the topmost snippet folder is selected (refer to
Figure 1.11).

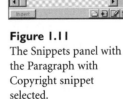

Figure 1.11
The Snippets panel with
the Paragraph with
Copyright snippet
selected.

11. Select the DWT_Delete snippet folder, and drag and drop it
onto the DWT snippet folder. Notice that the snippet folder and its contents
moved as you specified, without displaying a confirmation dialog. Keeping this in
mind, you can see how naming and organization is very important. You should
also be able to see why naming your snippets appropriately can be a real help.

12. Select the Paragraph with Copyright class snippet and drag it to the DWT snippet folder.

13. Select the DWT_Delete folder and press Delete, the Backspace key, or the Remove button.

14. When prompted with a confirmation message, click the Yes button to delete the folder.

15. Close any open documents and close DMX. This completes Exercise 1.1.

Share Your Snippets with Other Developers

You can share snippets three ways using DMX:

- Copy your snippets from the created folder and put them into a shared folder; then have your fellow developers copy them into their snippets folder and restart DMX. The shared folder can be a network shared folder or a site folder that you can name something like shared_snippets.

- Create a Snippet Extension and send your fellow developers the MXP file to have the Extension Manager install the snippets in the appropriate locations. (See the section later in this chapter, entitled "Building a Snippet Extension.")

- Use the Snippets Exchange to submit and distribute your favorite snippets. (See the section later in this chapter, entitled "The Snippet Exchange.")

Exercise 1.2: Sharing Snippets

Building on Exercise 1.1, let's share the created snippets with your fellow developers using a site folder. The most difficult part of this task is locating these custom snippets and their folders.

DMX on Windows and Mac stores many of the user customized settings in a different location than Dreamweaver/UltraDev 4 did. Dreamweaver/UltraDev 4 stored installed extensions and user settings at C:\Program Files\Macromedia\ APPLICATION\Configuration for Windows machines & DRIVE:Applications: Macromedia: APPLICATION:Configuration for Mac.

Well, that's all changed with DMX! Dreamweaver uses a new multiuser configuration, so now instead of looking in the previously easy-to-locate folders for your customizations, you need to look in C:\Documents and Settings\USERNAME\Application Data\ Macromedia\APPLICATION\Configuration for Windows machines and DRIVE:Users: USERNAME:Library:Application Support: Macromedia:APPLICATION:Configuration for Mac. This applies if your operating system supports the multiuser environment, such as Windows NT, 2000, XP, and OSX. If you're using a non-multiuser operating system such as Windows 98, ME, or OS 9.x, the previously mentioned folder locations apply.

It's beyond the scope of this book to explain the new support for a multiuser environment. If you want more information regarding this feature, suggested readings are the Extension Manager F1 help files and the book entitled, *Inside Dreamweaver MX*, by Laura Gutman et al (New Riders Publishing).

1. Open your file manager (Windows Explorer or Mac Finder).

2. Navigate to the DWTSI_Templates folder that you created with the other projects in this section and create a new subfolder named **Shared_Snippets**.

3. If you're working in a multiuser environment (Windows NT, 2000, XP, and OSX), navigate to C:\Documents and Settings\USERNAME\Application Data\Macromedia\Dreamweaver MX\Configuration\Snippets (in Windows) or DRIVE:Users:USERNAME:Library:Application Support: Macromedia: Dreamweaver MX:Configuration:Snippets (on the Mac).

   If you're working in a single-user environment (Windows 98, ME, and OS 9.1), navigate to C:\Program Files\Macromedia\Dreamweaver MX\ Configuration\Snippets (in Windows) or DRIVE:Applications: Macromedia:Dreamweaver MX:Configuration: (on the Mac).

4. Copy the DWT folder to the Shared_Snippets folder that you created in step 2. (Make sure that you copy the folder *and* contents—not only the two snippets inside—or your co-workers won't have the proper snippet folder structure.)

5. Upload your files to the server using any FTP program or Dreamweaver itself, ensuring that you do not cloak the Shared_Snippets folder. (See Chapter 6, "Building the Hot Cool Toys Base Template," for information on cloaking.) You could even zip this folder and email it to your co-workers with instructions (see step 6).

Note

Cloaking is the ability to hide a folder or file type from the ftp engine.

6. Contact your co-workers and tell them to download the newest version of the site, including the Shared_Snippets folder. Then tell them to perform the following:

   Copy the DWT folder from the Shared_Snippets folder in the site as follows:

   In a multiuser environment (Windows NT, 2000, XP, and OSX), navigate to C:\Documents and Settings\USERNAME\Application Data\Macromedia\ Dreamweaver MX\Configuration\Snippets (in Windows) or DRIVE:Users:USERNAME:Library:Application Support: Macromedia:Dreamweaver MX:Configuration:Snippets (on the Mac).

   In a single-user environment (Windows 98, ME, and OS 9.X), navigate to C:\Program Files\Macromedia\APPLICATION\Configuration\Snippets (in Windows) and DRIVE:Applications: Macromedia:APPLICATION:Configuration: (on the Mac).

7. Last, have your co-workers restart Dreamweaver. They should see the snippets and folder in their Snippet panel. The snippets should be ready to use.

8. Close your FTP application (or Dreamweaver, if you used that) and your file management application. This completes Exercise 1.2.

Build a Snippet Extension

Luckily, the Snippets panel is extensible! If you have a few favorites of your own that you want to share with friends or co-workers, it's as easy as building an extension for them and redistributing that extension. This happens to be the easiest way to share snippets. Fortunately, snippets have been added to the DMX Extensibility layer as a code snippet type in the Extension Manager. The important things here are configuring the MXI properly and copying the proper snippets for building the extension. We will outline these requirements next in Exercise 1.3.

Exercise 1.3:   Create a Snippet Extension

Building on Exercise 1.2, create a Snippet Extension to make it easy to share your favorite snippets.

It is beyond the scope of this book to cover all the details of building extensions, but this section gives you everything you need to create your own Snippet Extensions and distribute them to your co-workers.

1. Visit `www.dwteam.com/Extensions/` and download and save the MXI Doc Type extension to your local hard drive. Using Extension Manager, install the MXI Doc Type extension. (For extension installation instructions, please visit our support site at `www.dreamweavermx-templates.com/extensions.cfm`.) Close the Extension Manager.

2. Start DMX, making sure that you have the same site selected you used for Exercises 1.1 and 1.2 (DWTSI_Templates). Completion of Exercises 1.1 and 1.2 is a requirement of this exercise, so if you have not completed those exercises, please do so before you continue.

3. Select Edit > Preferences > File Types/Editors, and add .MXI to the field labeled Open in Code View. Click OK, and you now can create new MXI files and edit them by selection through the Site panel as with any other file type that you open from the site panel.

4. Using the Site panel, open the Extensions folder and open the file named My_Snippets.mxi.

```
<macromedia-extension
name="Name you wish to appear in Extension Manager"
version="1.0.0"
type="code snippet"
requires-restart="True">

<products>
     <product name="Dreamweaver" version="6" primary="true"
     required="true" />
</products>

<author name="Your name goes here" />

<description>
     <![CDATA[Description of Snippets Extension goes here.]]>
</description>

<ui-access>
     <![CDATA[Description of how to access the Snippets goes
        here.]]>
</ui-access>

<help-changes>
</help-changes>

<files>
     <file source=" " destination="$dreamweaver/Configuration/
     Snippets" />
     <file source=" " destination="$dreamweaver/Configuration/
     Snippets" />
</files>

<configuration-changes>
</configuration-changes>
</macromedia-extension>
```

5. Change line 2 (Extension Name—used by the Extension Manager) from
   `name="Name you wish to appear in Extension Manager"` to `name="Company`
   `Copyright Snippets"`.

6. Change line 11 (Author Name—used by the Extension Manager) from `<author`
   `name="Your name goes here" />` to `<author name="DWT" />`.

7. Change line 14 (Extension Description—used by the Extension Manager) from
   `<![CDATA[Description of Snippets Extension goes here.]]>` to
   `<![CDATA[This Snippet Extension inserts a new snippet folder`
   `labeled DWT and 2 copyright snippets.]]>`.

8. Change line 18 (Extension UI Access—used by Extension Manager) from
   `<![CDATA[Description of how to access the Snippets goes here.]]>` to
   `<![CDATA[Open the Snippets panel, select the DWT folder. Use the`
   `two snippets as outlined in the Snippet Description.]]>`.

9. At line 25, change (Source/Destination of snippet—used by the Extension Manager) from `<file source=" " destination="$dreamweaver/Configuration/Snippets" />` to `<file source="DWT\My Copyright.csn" destination="$dreamweaver/Configuration/Snippets/DWT" />`

10. At line 26, change (Source/Destination of snippet—used by the Extension Manager) from `<file source=" " destination="$dreamweaver/Configuration/Snippets" />` to `<file source="DWT\Paragraph with Copyright.csn" destination="$dreamweaver/Configuration/Snippets/DWT" />`

11. Select File > Save As, navigate to the site Shared_Snippets folder, change the filename to **Co_Copyright.mxi**, and click the Save button.

12. Close the document and close Dreamweaver.

13. Start the Extension Manager. You need the Extension Manager to package the files into an MXP file—an Extension Package file that contains all the files in a nice little archive.

14. Select File > Package Extension.

15. Navigate to the site root/Shared_Snippets folder and select the Co_Copyright.mxi file; then click OK.

16. The filename changes from Co_Copyright.mxi to Co_Copyright.mxp in this dialog; click the Save button.

17. If you typed everything perfectly as shown, the extension should be created without errors. If you received error messages, go back to step 1 and verify that you performed each step correctly.

    If you want to skip the MXI creation, we have included a completed MXI file named Co_Copyright.mxi in the site's Extensions folder. Simply open this file in Dreamweaver, save it in the Shared_Snippets folder, and then proceed to step 13.

18. Email the MXP to your co-workers, telling them to use the Extension Manager to install it.

19. Close any open documents and close the Extension Manager. This completes Exercise 1.3.

If you want or need to learn more about extending Dreamweaver either for snippets or for other items, please read *Dreamweaver MX Extensions* by Laura Gutman (New Riders Publishing, 2003).

Snippets Panel Advantages and Disadvantages

The advantages of using the Snippets panel include the following:

- Snippets are extensible in the sense that extensions can be built and used to share snippets between users.

- You can insert snippets by dragging and dropping them from the panel to the document.

- You can create subfolders for better organization of snippets.

- You can configure Snippet preview for Code or Design view.

- The snippets are not site specific

On the other hand, these are some of the negative aspects of the Snippets panel:

- You cannot import or export snippets to or from Homesite, Homesite+, JRun Studio, or ColdFusion Studio.

- Page-inserted snippets do not get updated when changes are made to them in the Snippets panel (as with Library items, for instance).

- There is no visual indicator that a snippet is Wrap or Block type, or Code or Design view specific.

Third-Party Snippet Options

Massimo Foti has created a couple of very useful extensions that are directly related to snippets. At the time of this writing, these are the only two snippet-related extensions available. Please check the Macromedia Exchange for updates or additions to this extensible layer.

The Snippet Converter by Massimo Foti

The Snippet Converter (see Figure 1.12) was built to allow customers of Classic Snippets Panel (formerly known as Snippets Panel) to convert their beloved snippets into DMX Snippets panel format. The conversion is "one-way only" but can be used repeatedly if you update your snippets in the other applications. The Snippet Converter also will convert your snippets from Homesite, Homesite+, ColdFusion Studio, and JRun Studio into the new DMX Snippets panel format (`www.dwfaq.com/Snippets/converter.asp`).

Figure 1.12   The Snippets Converter UI.

The Classic Snippets Panel Extension by Massimo Foti

In 2001, Massimo Foti introduced Classic Snippets Panel Extension (see Figure 1.13), which allows you to import into Dreamweaver 4 and/or UltraDev 4 snippets created with Homesite, ColdFusion Studio, and JRun Studio. This robust extension can be purchased for $45 (U.S.) at the Project Seven Web Store (`www.projectseven.com/viewer/snippets.htm`).

Figure 1.13
The Classic Snippets
Panel.

The extension includes an outstanding User Guide as well as 26 ready-to-use snippets. Because the User Guide is so well documented, we won't explain how to use it but rather explore the advantages and disadvantages of using the Classic Snippets Panel Extension.

Some advantages of Classic Snippets include the following:

- You can import and export snippets with Homesite, Homesite+, ColdFusion Studio, JRun Studio, Dreamweaver 4.x, and UltraDev 4.x. (This is possible only if the Classic Snippets Panel Extension has been installed.) This means that you can then set up the other applications to use the Classic Snippets Panel snippets folder as their Shared snippets folder by using the programs' Preferences, Configuration, or Options commands. When you do this, any new snippets in any of the applications will be recognized application-wide.

- Includes 26 pre-built snippets.

- Includes a User Guide that is second to none.

- Extensible, in the sense that extensions can be built and used to share snippets between users.

These are some disadvantages of Classic Snippets:

- You cannot import snippets from the DMX Snippets panel.

- You cannot export snippets to the DMX Snippets panel. (This disadvantage is overcome by the use of the free Snippets Converter Extension by Massimo Foti.)

- Page-inserted snippets do not get updated when changes are made to them in the Classic Snippets Panel (as they are with DMX snippets).

- There is no visual indicator that a Snippet is Wrap or Block type, or Code or Design view specific.

- Classic Snippets is a retail product, so you will have to outlay a pittance of cash if you really want it. (It's actually under-priced for the amount of work that went into it to provide the functionality that it has).

The Snippets Exchange

The brainchild of Massimo Foti and implemented by Daniel Short and Angela C. Buraglia (www.dwfaq.com/Snippets/default.asp), the Snippets Exchange is just that—a place where you can submit and/or download snippets for your DMX Snippets panel and the Classic Snippets Panel (see Figure 1.14). Originally this site was built to hold and support the Classic Snippets panel, because it was created prior to DMX. With the release of DMX, the site now generates both required sets of files (.csn for DMX and .hss and .hse for Dreamweaver/UltraDev 4) and updates whichever panel you have in Dreamweaver/UltraDev 4 and DMX.

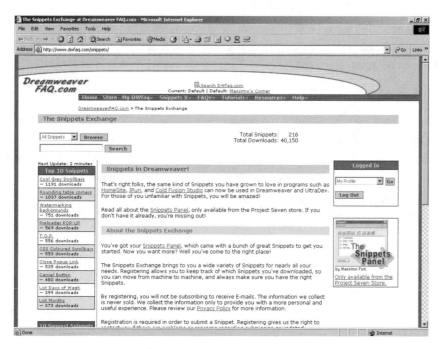

Figure 1.14   The Snippets Exchange.

Interview: Angela C. Buraglia

Angela C. Buraglia —
Dreamweaver FAQ

Business Name: DreamweaverFAQ

URL: www.dreamweaverfaq.com

Who are you and what do you do?

I'm a mother, wife, web developer, writer, tech editor, and one of those people who have a difficult time answering questions like this one! I am also the founder of DreamweaverFAQ.com and a Team Macromedia volunteer for Dreamweaver.

Do you use snippets in your development?

I've been using snippets ever since Massimo introduced me to the concept in August of 2001. Before that time, I would browse to a file I knew used the code I needed, and then I would copy it and paste it into the current document. Now, I couldn't imagine development without snippets!

Do you find that snippets help or hinder workflow?

Snippets definitely lend a hand in the speed of my workflow. The only way a snippet itself could hinder workflow is if it was difficult to find. Naming your snippets intuitively and storing them logically is very important. It is also a good idea to test the code before—and in some cases even after—making it a snippet so that when it comes time to use it, you won't get unexpected results that may slow you down.

What brought about the Snippets Exchange?

When Massimo Foti developed his original version of the Classic Snippets panel, he approached me to host the Snippets Exchange at DreamweaverFAQ.com. He knew it would be a big job and had confidence in Daniel Short, DWfaq's ASP guru, to do the development. We knew that people would want to fill up their panel with useful snippets, and that many Dreamweaver users new to the concept of snippets could use a resource such as the Snippets Exchange to help them do that.

What is your favorite snippet?

That's such a tough question! Often I need to nest a table within another table to create an outlined appearance in the browser. I have made a snippet that will wrap the current selection (in this case, an entire table) with the necessary table tags and formatting. I have several variations of this snippet and find myself using it more than most of my others.

Summary

Snippets can be an important tool you use as you develop your web sites. This chapter acquainted you with snippets and the basics of their structure, use, and possibilities. ∎

Chapter 2

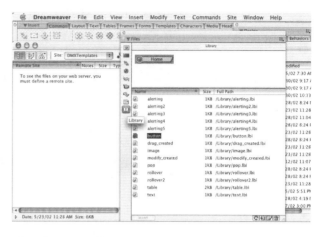

The Library panel.

Library Items
Revealed

Combining templates with library items gives you a tremendous amount of flexibility in building a complex site. In this chapter, you learn about the power that library items can bring to the developer's toolkit.

What Are Library Items?

Think of a library item as a mini-template without defined regions. As such, it is a design-time tool that provides the benefit of automatically updating all pages on which it has been used, but without the complexity of templates.

Library items give you the ability to insert and reuse snippets of specific page content (code), such as a menu. Dreamweaver tracks each instance of an inserted library item so that whenever a library item is modified, this modification is propagated to all pages using that library item. In Chapter 1 you learned about snippets, and the major feature that distinguishes a library item from a snippet is this tracking and propagation of changes.

Library items are intended for use within the `<body>` tags of a page. If you want to insert reusable code into a page's `<head>` area, then read Chapter 1 on snippets. Attempting to use library items within the `<head>` area of a document can produce puzzling and unpleasant results.

Similar to snippets, a library item in its simplest form can be a single letter suitable for display on a web page—for example, it would be possible to make a library item from the Icelandic letter "thorn" (Þ). `You can also save a complete web page's body content (including menu interactivity and other advanced features) as a library item.

To summarize, library items represent fragments of a page. As such, a library item should not contain `<html></html>`, `<head></head>`, or `<body></body>` tag pairs (just as with server-side includes); otherwise, the receiving page may have unintended duplication of these tags, with attendant problems. DMX has refined the algorithms for creating library items so that the possibility of this happening is minimized.

Despite the obvious appeal and utility of library items, they can be confusing to use. This chapter attempts to dispel some of this confusion.

Methods of Creating Libraries

First you need to understand what the library is and where it resides. The library is a folder (named *Library*, not surprisingly), whose contents are counted as an asset by Dreamweaver. The folder is listed within the Library section of the Assets panel. Within this folder are files, each of which is named with the *.lbi (library item) extension (refer to Table 3.1 in Chapter 3). These files contain the text that is to be reused within this site and is produced whenever a new library item is created.

To prepare for the next discussion, open the Library section of the Asset panel by selecting Window > Assets (F11) and clicking the Library icon on the left of the panel at the bottom of the icon list.

> **Note**
>
> Do not rename or move the Library folder outside the root folder of the site; otherwise, the propagation feature of library items will not work correctly. Renaming or moving the Library folder breaks the link between the library item and the page containing it, which obviously removes much of its potential utility.

The Library folder is not created in your site until the first library item is created. Once it has been created in a site, this folder remains even if you subsequently delete all library items.

You create a library item by selecting content in a document and placing it in the library, using one of the following methods:

- Drag and drop the selected content onto the Library panel. This action produces an unnamed file in the library and positions the cursor so that you can name the file. The action also converts the selected content (that is, the code in the page that was dragged and dropped) into a reference to the newly created file in the Library.

- Select Modify > Library > Add Object to library, and continue as in the first bullet item.

- Click the New Library Item icon at the bottom of the Library panel and continue as in the first bullet item.

- Using the context menu in the Assets panel, right-click (Control+click) in the library listing area and choose New Library Item from the menu.

- In addition to the above methods, you can create a library item "outside" Dreamweaver's library user interface by saving a file with an .lbi extension in the Library folder.

- Choose File > New and select Basic Page and Library Item to create the library item from scratch.

> **Note**
>
> Be aware that this last method does not automatically create the Library folder; nor does it automatically save the new library item into the Library folder if it already exists. This means that you must manually create the Library folder or save the new library item into the existing Library folder.

Any of these methods will produce good results as long as you are not relying on custom code located external to the source for the library item; in that case, special precautions must be taken. See the section, "Advantages and Disadvantages," later in this chapter for a discussion regarding the use of custom JavaScript with library items.

You can identify the library item's code on a page in several ways. In Design view and Code view, the library item is shown with a highlighted background color, as you specified in the preferences you select. (You can set the value for background color in Design view by choosing Edit > Preferences > Highlighting; and for Code view, choose Edit > Preferences > Code Coloring.). In addition, each instance of the code for a library item is contained in code similar to this:

```
<!-- #BeginLibraryItem "/Library/text.lbi" -->
<p>I am text</p><!-- #EndLibraryItem -->
```

Note

If a library item contains only an image reference or a swf reference, Design view may not show a highlight around that object (the highlighting is still there, but sometimes is not visible). Code view will display this highlighting properly, however.

When you select a library item on the page (even while in Code view), the Library item Property inspector appears, if the Property inspector is onscreen as determined by the Window > Properties menu item. Note that if the library item is in a locked region, you will have to open the parent template to have any library item control.

Library Item Code Coloring

You can customize Dreamweaver library item code coloring to your preferences. The customization affects all code starting at the opening library markup and finishing at the end of the closing library markup.

The unfortunate part is that there are several locations at which to change the coloring. You can choose a color setting for each document type and one for nested library items. Here we describe the method to change the HTML library item coloring and to set the nested library item coloring. The other document types are very similar, although the selections may differ slightly.

HTML Document Type Library Items

To access the HTML document type code coloring, select Edit > Preferences. Select the Code Coloring category (see Figure 2.1), choose the HTML Document Type, and click the Edit Coloring Scheme button. This brings up the Edit Coloring Scheme dialog, as you see in Figure 2.2.

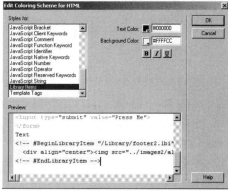

Figure 2.1   The Edit > Preferences dialog.   **Figure 2.2**   The Edit Color Scheme dialog.

Scroll down the Styles for list and select Library Items. You can change the style for the Library Item by adding bold, italic, or underline, as well as changing the text and/or background color. These changes affect the display of library item code in Code view only.

The changes you make here apply to library items in HTML and HTML Template documents in Code view only. Because there is no reset color scheme button and you may want to return the defaults to their original settings at some point in the future, we have listed the default settings for your convenience in Table 2.1. One last thing to note is that the Preview field of this dialog is not a live display, which means that it does not visually represent any changes you make and has no easy provision to add a library item so that you can see the result of your changes.

Table 2.1   Code Coloring Defaults

Heading	Setting
Text Color	#000000
Background Color	#FFFFCC
Bold	Deselected
Italic	Deselected
Underline	Deselected

Tip

It is beyond the scope of this book to show you how to edit the preview file, but if you're interested, look for a file named CodeColoring.xml in your user profile settings at `Macromedia\Dreamweaver MX\Configuration\CodeColoring`. (To learn more about Dreamweaver MX's file locations, start the Extension Manager, press F1, and choose help on "Installing and managing extensions in multi-user environments > The configuration folders").

Library Item Document Type Library Items (Nested)

To access the library item document type code coloring, select Edit > Preferences. Select the Code Coloring category (see Figure 2.3). Next, select the Library Item Document Type; then select the Edit Coloring Scheme button. This brings up the Edit Coloring Scheme dialog as seen in Figure 2.4. Scroll down the Styles for list and select Library Items. Similarly to HTML Document Type, you can change the style for the Library Item by adding Bold, Italics, or Underline, as well as changing the text and/or background color. These changes affect the display of library item code in Code view only.

Note

The changes you make here apply to library items in library items (in other words, nested) in Code View only. There is no reset color scheme button, so we have listed the default settings for your convenience in Table 2.2. One last thing to note is that the Preview field of this dialog is not a live display, does not visually represent any changes you make, and does not allow you to add a library item so that you can see the changes.

Tip

It is beyond the scope of this book to show you how to edit the preview file, but if you're interested, have a look through your user profile settings at Macromedia\Dreamweaver MX\Configuration\CodeColoring for a file named CodeColoring.xml. (To learn more about Dreamweaver MX's file locations, start the Extension Manager, press F1, and choose help on "Installing and managing extensions in multi-user environments > The configuration folders".)

Table 2.2   Code Coloring Defaults

Heading	Setting
Text Color	#000000
Background Color	#FFFFCC
Bold	Deselected
Italic	Deselected
Underline	Deselected

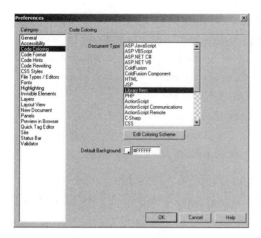

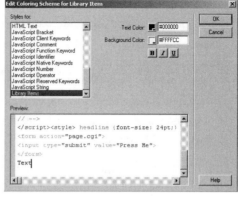

Figure 2.3   Edit > Preferences dialog.   **Figure 2.4**   Edit Color Scheme dialog.

Highlighting Options

You can change the highlighting colors and visibility in the Edit > Preferences dialog
using the Highlighting category (see Figure 2.5). This area and the View menu's Visual
Aids > Invisible Elements command work hand in hand.

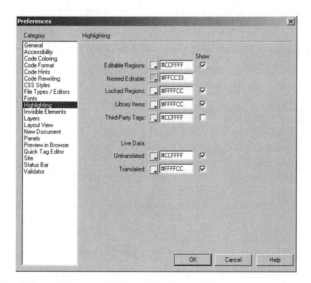

Figure 2.5   The Edit > Preferences dialog with the Highlighting category selected.

As you can see in the figure, several options are available in this category. You are concerned with only one in this chapter: Library Items. Note that this preference affects
only Design view display.

The specific selection pair shown on the Preferences Panel when you have selected the Highlighting Category (i.e., the columns containing a color pad and a Show checkbox) enables you to control the display of library items defined in HTML documents, template files and nested library items, as well as those carried through to child pages of an HTML template. By clicking to remove the checkmark in the Show field, you keep the library item highlighting from appearing on the editor pages, which makes it very difficult to know where you have used a library item. The color is used as a highlight for the library item. The default values are #FFFFCC and Show Checked.

In order to see the highlighting for library item markup, you must make sure View > Visual Aids > Invisible Elements is enabled. If it is not checked, only Code view will highlight the library item. Note that this menu selection is not global; instead, you must enable or disable it for each document that you open.

Methods of Editing Library Items

Although you can edit library items by directly modifying the code in a containing page's Code view, it is always safest to open the library item separately and make modifications to the library item directly rather than changing an instance of the library item. Note that if the library item is in a locked region, you will have to open the parent template to actually have any library item control. Save your work carefully when you are first creating library items if the item's parent document is also open. While we were testing, we found that sometimes the expected prompt to save the parent document does not appear.

> **Note**
> When you remove a library item from a template, the changes will affect all files associated with that template after it is saved. This means that if you remove the library item from the template, you should save the changes to the template and update the associated pages so that the change will propagate to your child pages.

When you select a library item in a containing page, you can open an item for editing it several ways:

- Right-click the library item to open the context menu and choose Open Library Item (only in Design view, however). As mentioned earlier, if the library item is in a locked region, you will have to open the parent template to actually have any library item control.
- Left-click the Open button on the Library Item Property inspector. The same restrictions apply regarding locked regions, as mentioned previously.

- Right-click or double-click the library item in the Library panel and select Edit.

- Select the library item and then click the Edit icon at the bottom of the Library panel.

- Double-click the file in the Library folder in the Site Manager.

Any of these methods will open the library item in a separate document window and allow you to edit all associated code.

 Note

You can insert another library item while editing a library item, which means that you can nest library items. Although the full depth of this nesting—and especially the point at which is may become problematic for a site—still needs to be fully explored, the fact that it can be done at all brings up some interesting possibilities.

Methods of Using Library Items

You can use multiple methods to insert, or use, library items. You can drag and drop them on the page, insert them by right-clicking (Ctrl+click) the library item in the Assets panel and choosing Insert, or add them using the Insert button at the bottom of the Library panel. Curiously, there is no corresponding Insert menu option in Dreamweaver.

 Note

After you use the Insert button to add a library item to a page, the item is selected and the Insert button is disabled until you deselect the library item. Note also that if you use the drag-and-drop method, the Insert button has no bearing whether it is enabled or disabled.

After the item is placed on the page, Dreamweaver will maintain this library item just as it does with changes to Non-Editable Regions in a Template page.

 Tip

Interestingly, you can even recursively nest library items; that is, a library item can be nested within itself. Although Dreamweaver displays a message about not being able to update the parent file, the program ignores the warning and makes the change anyway— even though the inner nest has lost its linking to the parent library item!

Deleting a Library Item

Deleting a library item from a page is very simple. Open the page in Dreamweaver, click the library item in Design view, and press Delete. This removes the instance of that library item from that page, but the item is not removed from the Library. Note that if the library item is in a locked region, you will have to open the parent template to actually have any library item control.

Alternatively, you can remove a library item from a page by selecting it in the Design view of the containing page and clicking the Detach from Original button on the Property inspector. This method removes the link to the library item from the page, but will leave the content of the library item on the page. Note that if the library item is in a locked region, you will have to open the parent template to actually have any library item control.

In order to remove the library item permanently from the Library, do one of the following:

- Select the library item file by name in the Library panel, and click the trash icon on the lower part of the panel.
- Right-click the file in the Assets panel and select Delete.
- Select the file in the Assets panel or the Site Manager and press Delete.

Warning

Throughout our combined experience, we have found that using any of these methods other than the first one to permanently delete library items has produced unexpected results with the site cache's tracking of links in both DW and DMX. This required us to rebuild both the Asset cache and the Site cache several times.

Re-Creating a Library Item

Occasionally, the link between a page's library item and the parent file gets broken. This can happen when the file defining a library item is deleted from the Library. In this case, it is easy to re-establish this link by opening the page, selecting the library item, and using one of the following ways to re-create the link:

- Click the Recreate button on the Property inspector. Note that if the library item is in a locked region, you will have to open the parent template to actually have any library item control.

- Right-click and select Recreate from the context menu. Note that if the library item is in a locked region, you will have to open the parent template to actually have any library item control.

Either of these methods restores function to the "orphaned" library item.

Updating a Library Item

What happens when you make a modification to your library item and then elect *not* to update the page? As with many other things, you can do it later!

You can use two methods to update a page or an entire site. Each method requires that a page in the site that uses the library item be open.

The Modify Menu System

When you select Modify > Library, you see two choices. The first choice is Update Current Page. When you select this option, the library item(s) on the current page are checked against the library and updated as needed without warning or confirmation. The only indication you get that the job is done is that the document is given focus for editing.

The other option is Update Pages. When you select this menu item, the Update Pages dialog opens (see Figure 2.6). Here you can choose to update the entire site, or you can update selected files containing a specific library item that you choose in the Look in fields. Ensure that Library Items is checked and leave Templates unchecked. By leaving Templates unchecked and checking Library Items, you are telling the interface to worry only about updating pages that contain the changed library item (template or not). The Templates checkbox is explored in Chapter 3, "All About Templates and Regions." You can have the dialog also show you the log of modified files when it is finished processing by enabling this box. Disabling this box hides the status window from view in the dialog.

The Library Assets Context Menu

The Library Assets panel context menu can be used to access the same functions as the Modify > Library menu choices as detailed in the previous section. Functionality and dialogs are identical—the difference comes in with the names and accessibility of the options.

Both are accessed via the Assets panel, Library context menu. The two menu selections you are concerned with here are Update Current Page and Update Site. Notice that there is a naming convention difference here but the functionality is identical.

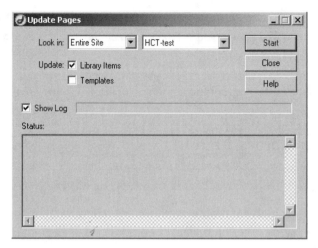

Figure 2.6   The Update Pages dialog.

Note

When you are using Update Current Page and the library item to be updated is in a non-editable region of a child page, it does not get updated. This happens because it is in a locked region. To update this library item, you need to open the template file and then select any of these menu items.

Design Time Style Sheets

Macromedia was obviously thinking about developers when they built this little gem of a feature into Dreamweaver MX. Design time style sheets fit perfectly with library items.

You may have noticed that your CSS files are not accessible when you are creating or modifying a library item. Until now, the only option you had was to memorize your CSS and manually assign the classes within your library items, or alternatively, to re-create your library item from the source HTML file each time you wanted to do an update to a tag. Thanks to design time style sheets, this is no longer the case.

With design time style sheets, you can attach a style sheet to a specific document (a library item is a perfect example). The style sheet is attached only to that document so that you can assign classes via the CSS menu to content within the document that is referencing that design time style sheet. The design time style sheet is visible only when you are in Design view and does not affect uploaded pages, so make sure that you properly attach the style sheet to the HTML document containing the library item. OK, you're pumped and wanting to give this a try. Exercise 2.1 walks you through the use of design time style sheets as they relate to library items.

Exercise 2.1:   Using Design Time Style Sheets with Library Items

Library items cannot have cascading style sheets directly associated with them, so apply-ing styles inside library items is problematic at best. Macromedia has developed a won-derful solution to this issue with the Design Time Style Sheets option, which you explore in this exercise.

1. Make sure your site is defined and Dreamweaver is open.

Note

It's assumed that you have the required site defined in DMX and that Dreamweaver is running. If not, then please see the instructions provided in the section entitled "Defining Your Site" in the Section 1 Introduction, or start Dreamweaver if your site is already defined.

2. In the Site panel, click the (+) beside the Library folder to expand the folder list-ing, and open the library item named dtcss.lbi by double-clicking it. The library item should populate the document window at this point.

3. Select File > Design Notes to open the Design Notes dialog as seen in Figure 2.7.

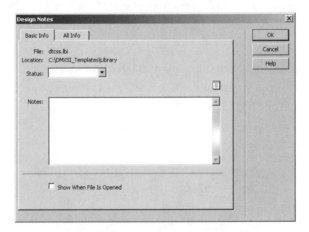

Figure 2.7   The Design Notes dialog.

4. Now, click the All Info tab at the top of the dialog and notice that the dialog is empty except for the control buttons and labels. In other words, no notes are defined (see Figure 2.8).

5. Click OK to accept changes or Cancel to abandon changes. Because you didn't make any changes to the notes for this document, either choice is fine.

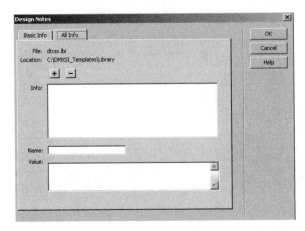

Figure 2.8   The Design Notes dialog, with the All Info tab displayed.

6. Display the Design Time Style Sheets dialog one of two ways:

- From the menu, select Text > CSS Styles > Design Time Style Sheets and the dialog appears as long as there is a document open and the document has been saved. (If the document is a new, untitled document, the menu entry is disabled.)

- When your document is displayed in Design view, click the right mouse button (Ctrl+click) to bring up the context menu; then choose CSS Styles > Design Time Style Sheets.

Using either of these methods displays the Design Time Style Sheets dialog as seen in Figure 2.9.

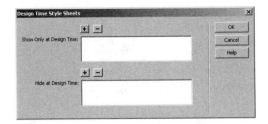

Figure 2.9   The Design Time Style Sheets dialog.

7. The dialog interface is simple to use. There are two fields: the top labeled Show Only at Design Time and the bottom labeled Hide at Design Time. Each of these fields has two control buttons, a plus (+) and a minus (−). The (+) button displays another dialog that is used to assign style sheets to either field (depending on which (+) button you click) as seen in Figure 2.10.

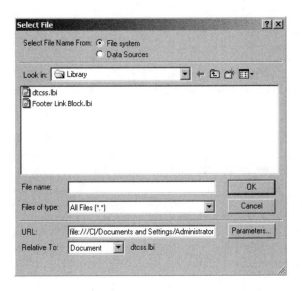

Figure 2.10   The Select File dialog.

The (–) button will remove the currently selected style sheet from the Design Time dialog.

Using method 1, select Text > CSS Styles > Design Time Style Sheets. When the dialog appears, select the (+) button at the top of the Show at Design Time field to open the Select File dialog. Navigate to the site root (DWXSI_Templates) and select the file named work.css (see Figure 2.11). Make sure that the Relative To field shows Document and not Site Root, or you could have problems assigning classes to your document.

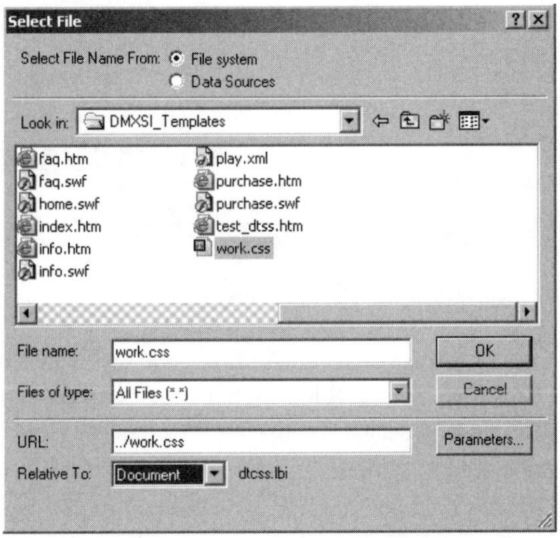

Figure 2.11   The completed Select File dialog.

8. Click OK. This causes the selected css file to be accessible for the library item document that is currently open.

9. The Design Time Style Sheets dialog will have the previously selected CSS file listed in the Show at Design Time field, as you see in Figure 2.12. Click the OK button on the Design Time Style Sheets dialog to complete the process and close the dialog.

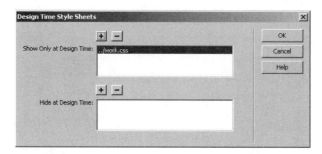

Figure 2.12   The completed Design Time Style Sheet dialog.

10. Select File > Design Notes to open the Design Notes dialog. Now, click the All Info tab at the top of the dialog and notice that the dialog has two new records in it (see Figure 2.13).

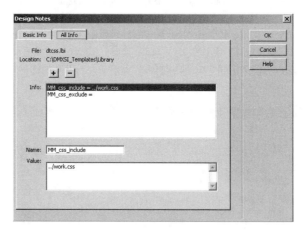

Figure 2.13   Design Notes Dialog – All Info tab displayed

11. MM_css_include contains the assigned list of style sheets that will be accessible at design time, and MM_css_exclude contains the assigned list of style sheets to be ignored at design time. Click OK to close the dialog.

12. In the open document, select the word Design, right-click (Ctrl+click) it to bring up the context menu, and select CSS Styles. In the list that appears, choose

the design class. Notice that the application of the class is immediate and there is no real CSS file attached to this document other than the design time style sheet.

13. Repeat step 8, using the words *Time* and *Style Sheets*, selecting classes of time and sheet, respectively. Your final library item should look like Figure 2.14.

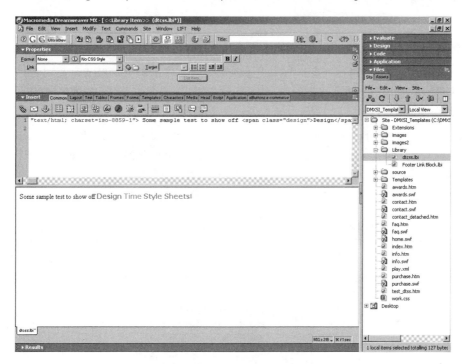

Figure 2.14   Completed exercise using design time style sheets.

Note

Notice that although there is no reference to the style sheet in the library item, we are able to access the classes and CSS specification of work.css within our library item by using design time style sheets.

14. Close all open documents.

You might wonder how Dreamweaver keeps track of which files have which design time sheets assigned or excluded. Well, like many other things, Dreamweaver stores this information in the document's notes file in the _notes folder. To see how the information is referenced, right-click (Ctrl+click) the file named dtcss.lbi in the Library folder of the DMXSI_Templates folder and choose Design Notes. Click the All Notes tab at the top and you will see two new fields (MM_css_include and MM_css_exclude). The first, MM_css_include, specifies which CSS file(s) are assigned to this document, and the other, MM_css_exclude, specifies which CSS file(s) are ignored by this document.

There are a couple of caveats to be aware of when using these little beauties. For instance, a file must be saved before you can assign the design time style sheet. Also, you must remember to link the style sheet to the base document that uses the library item or the class assignments won't display when they are previewed or viewed live on the web.

Miscellaneous Library Item Options

The Library panel is a subset of the Assets panel group. It contains a listing of the salient details of a site's Library files (name, size, and full path) as well as controlling icons and menu options.

At the bottom of the panel is a set of four context-sensitive icons. From left to right, these allow you to Refresh the Site List, Create a New Library Item, Edit the currently selected library item, and Delete (trash) the selected library item. Above the Site list is a preview pane, in which a preview (if any would be appropriate) of the selected library item is displayed.

At the top-right corner of the Library panel is a panel menu containing (and duplicating) many of the options available in other menus and icons when you are working with library items (see Figure 2.15).

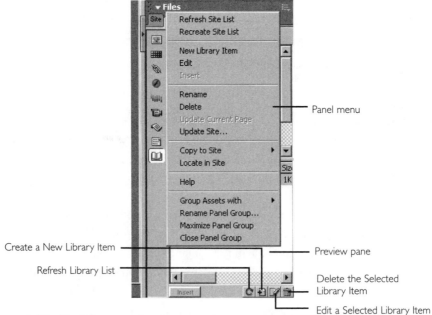

Figure 2.15   The Library panel and menu options.

Advantages and Disadvantages

Similar to any other tool, library items have advantages and disadvantages. The major advantages are related to the mini-parent/child updating of derived pages. The major disadvantage is related to the potential for confusion, error, and redundant code.

For example, consider the following simple page:

```
<html>
<head>
<title>Library Items</title>
<script language="JavaScript1.2">
<!--
function MM_popupMsg(msg) { //v1.0
  alert(msg);
}
//-->
</script>
</head>
<body>
<p><a href="javascript:;" onClick="MM_popupMsg('BOO')">LINK</a></p>
</body>
</html>
```

This page displays a single text link (LINK). When this link is clicked, a system alert containing BOO appears. If the word LINK is selected on this page in DMX and a library item is created either by selecting the Modify > Library > Add Object To Library command or by dragging and dropping it in the Library panel, the resulting library item looks like this:

```
<a href="javascript:;" onClick="MM_popupMsg('BOO')">LINK</a>
```

Depending on how your DMX is configured, you may also see the following line—or something similar—at the top of the library item's code:

```
<meta http-equiv="Content-Type" content="text/html; charset=iso-8859-1">
```

> **Note**
>
> The library item will reflect any Regional settings currently in effect for its parent document or for the default document. In the case of this example, the parent document was regionalized for typical western character sets; hence the ISO-8859-1 designation.

Note that the supporting JavaScript function is not taken into the library item:

```
<script language="JavaScript1.2">
<!--
function MM_popupMsg(msg) { //v1.0
  alert(msg);
}
//-->
</script>
```

That's OK, because when DMX inserts this library item into a new page, it also knows how to insert the supporting JavaScript. This means that, for example, if a new page is created and then used as the destination for this library item, the MM_popupMsg function definition will magically appear in the <head> area of this new file.

Potential confusion (and error) may arise when custom JavaScript is associated with the library item. For example, compare the preceding example with this following one:

```
<title>Custom Javascript</title>
<script language="JavaScript1.2">
<!--
function goalert(msg){
  alert(msg);
}
//-->
</script>
</head>

<body>
<p><a href="javascript:goalert();">LINK</a></p>
</body>
</html>
```

The only difference between these two example pages is that the former contains a DMX standard behavior (MM_popupMessage) and the latter contains a custom (although identical) JavaScript function (goalert). Creating a library item from the latter page (just as was done with the former page) creates this:

```
<meta  http-equiv="Content-Type"  content="text/html;  charset=iso-8859-
1"><a href="javascript:goalert('BOO');">LINK</a>
```

Again, nearly the same as the former example.

But because DMX has no idea what the goalert() function really *is*, when this library item is inserted onto a new page, the function definition is missing, as you see here:

```
<html>
<head>
<title>Custom Javascript2</title>
</head>

<body>
<!-- #BeginLibraryItem "/Library/alerting2.lbi" --><a
href="javascript:goalert();">LINK</a> <!-- #EndLibraryItem -->
</body>
</html>
```

Previewing this page in Internet Explorer 5.1 (with Javascript error messages enabled) will produce the error message shown in Figure 2.16.

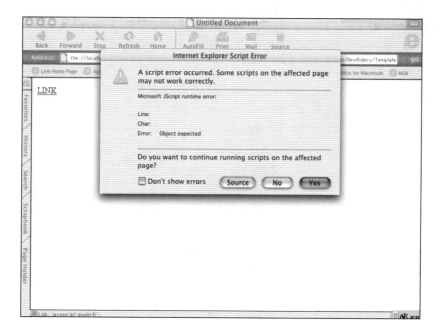

Figure 2.16   Error message caused by having a Javascript function call on a page, without having the corresponding function definition.

This error will be avoided if the receiving page already contains that goalert() JavaScript function in the HEAD. In other words, it is prudent to be cautious when using library items with custom or third-party JavaScript code.

A secondary and much less problematic issue with library files is the fact that they are considered dependent files when you upload your site to a remote host. This means that every library item parent file referenced in every page you upload will also be uploaded to your remote site. Because library items exert their effect only at design time, there is really no reason to upload these files, except in the event that you would want others to download them, as in a collaborative development environment. Fortunately, DMX allows you to avoid this by enabling cloaking for the Library folder. You will discover more about cloaking in Chapter 6, "Building the Hot Cool Toys Base Template."

Summary

Library items are important tools for web site developers, enabling you to update content on pages easily. This chapter introduced you to library items and explored their structure, use, and possibilities.   ∎

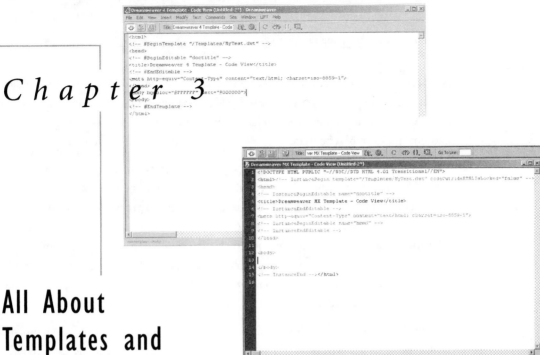

Chapter 3

All About Templates and Regions

Before and After.

The web site for Hot Cool Toys (Section II

project), which you will build by working

through the following chapters, is based

on DMX's templates, library items, and

snippets and their various capabilities. The versatility of these tools enables you to adapt a complex site for different page layout needs and maintain that site easily. This chapter introduces these tools, describes their functions and applications, and explains where and how they can best be used.

The function of a template is based on the properties of two specific regions of code in the HTML page: non-editable and editable regions. The basic mantra of templates is this: Changes made to a template's non-editable region will propagate to all child pages. Changes made to a template's editable region propagate *only* to new child pages created after those changes were made, and not to existing child pages of the same template. In a child page, non-editable regions are not editable, and editable regions are editable, which allows each child page to display unique content. There is no "back-propagation" of editable region content from child to parent.

You need to keep a few guidelines in mind any time you are considering using templates or library items in DMX or earlier versions. Templates and library items are saved in a special location within your local site—the Templates and Library folders, respectively (see Figure 3.1).

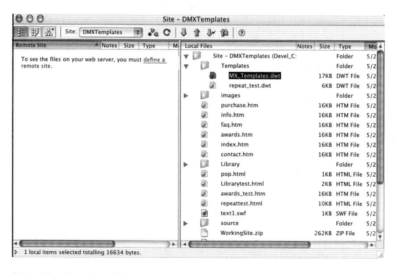

Figure 3.1   The Templates folder.

In order to preserve the automatic propagation of changes from parent to child…

- These folders must not be renamed
- These folders must not be moved from their location at the root level of the site.

- These folders should not contain anything (subfolders, images, databases, or other web page types and objects) other than files using the filename extension of .dwt (in the Templates folder) and .lbi (in the Library folder).

What good are rules if you cannot break them? Although the first two guidelines are important, as stated, for the propagation of changes, both can be broken. Doing so means that you must manually update the site after you make changes to either templates or library items, by selecting Modify > {Library/Templates} > Update Pages. Because the purpose of using these elements is to make creating and maintaining sites easier, we suggest you avoid breaking this rule unless your site structure demands it.

Note

Because the purpose of using these library/template elements is to make creating and maintaining sites easier, we suggest you avoid breaking this guideline unless your site structure or server/workflow architecture demands it.

The last guideline listed in the previous list is based on our experience with templates and library items. Many a person has asked for support when their child pages didn't update properly and it was determined that they had stored and referenced other file types from within the Templates or Library folders.

Given the folder location mentioned earlier, it is easy to recognize template files in your Site Manager display—they are always in the Templates folder! In addition, there is a specific nomenclature for template files.

In Dreamweaver, this template nomenclature used the file extension .dwt, as in FOO.DWT. In DMX, this file-naming convention is changed to one that inserts the dwt prior to the closing extension, which is selected depending on the type of child file the template is likely to produce. For example, an ASP template file might be named FOO.DWT.ASP; a JSP template file might be named FOO.DWT.JSP. See Table 3.1 for a comprehensive list of possible template filename extensions.

Table 3.1   File Extension Nomenclature

File Extension	Meaning
.dwt	Dreamweaver template (non-dynamic pages only)
.dwt.asp	Dreamweaver ASP template (new to MX)
.dwt.aspx	Dreamweaver .NET template (new to MX)
.dwt.cfm	Dreamweaver CF template (new to MX)
.dwt.jsp	Dreamweaver JSP template (new to MX)

Table 3.1   Continued

File Extension	Meaning
.dwt.php	Dreamweaver PHP template (new to MX)
.csn	Code Snippet (new to MX)
.hse	Homesite Snippet End code
.hss	Homesite Snippet Start code
.lbi	Library Item
.mxi	Macromedia Extension Information file
.mxp	Macromedia Extension Package

 Note

This change in file naming was implemented to prevent the security risk that might occur when a DW template file for a data-driven page was found on the server. Because the extension for this file is dwt, the server would not recognize it as containing any server-side code and would pass the file, unprocessed, to the requesting browser. This would mean that all server-side code would be revealed in the fetched .dwt file, which clearly presents a problem. By placing the .dwt as the penultimate extension, and by using a server-side file extension as the ultimate filename extension, all DMX templates will be stripped of server-side code before being offered in response to the fetch request.

In DW and DMX, the most frequent operational order for working with templates is to create a template page first, and then spawn child pages from these template parents. You can also retroactively apply templates to pages by using Modify > Templates > Apply Template To Page, which is covered later in this chapter. The reciprocal option to detach a page from a template is explored in detail in Chapter 4, "Removing Dreamweaver Markup."

Templates—the Good, the Bad, and the Ugly

Here's a lowdown of the pros and cons of templates:

Good	Ease of site maintenance
Bad	Has a steep learning curve
	Must upload all changed files to the server
	Can be very complex and include lots of additional code

Ugly   Consists of proprietary code

After a Fireworks-exported HTML page is converted
to a template and the various regions are added,
round-tripping (moving a file between Fireworks,
Dreamweaver, and Fireworks again) becomes problematic.

File links or references in server code, JavaScript, and
template parameters are not adjusted automatically

Design-Time versus Server-Side

Templates are design-time tools, meaning that they exert their influence only while the
files are sitting on your hard drive. Uploading a template file to the server has no effect
on any files already mounted on the server, nor will it affect any local files from that location. The only reason to upload a template file is to share it.

Server-side `includes` are much simpler to use than templates in the sense that there is
minimal special processing code added to your pages (as opposed to the often volumi-
nous DMX template directives and parameter specifications). Because server-side
`includes` are written into the document as it is being fetched from the server, a single
change to a single `include` file could express itself instantly site-wide, by simply changing the `include` file and then uploading it. Contrast this with the need to upload every
file that has been changed by modifying a single template file.

A potential difficulty with server-side `includes` is the need to ensure that the `include` is
truly a fragment of code. It ordinarily cannot contain <html>, <head>, or <body> tags;
otherwise, unexpected things may happen in the receiving page.

Remember that with `includes`, when you upload the `'include'` file, its changes propagate immediately.

Your strategy for site construction might contain the use of both the template and SSI
methods.

Site Maintenance Benefits and Strategies

Some benefits of using these elements to enhance your site maintenance include

- Ease of changes site-wide or section-wide in your web site
- Efficiency is increased over having unique pages on the site
- Site maintains a layout consistency

To make sure that your site is well-maintained, we suggest the following:

- Incorporate your changes in the template(s)
- Apply changes to the pages
- Upload all changed pages

Template Code Coloring

You can customize the appearance of template markup three different ways: by using code coloring, highlighting, or visual aids. These features work in concert, and they are discussed individually in the following sections.

Code Coloring

You can apply a unique color to the region code, including the opening region comment and the closing region comment, by choosing Edit > Preferences > Code Coloring (see Figure 3.2). In this category, select the HTML Document Type and click the Edit Coloring Scheme button. This brings up the Edit Coloring Scheme dialog, as you see in Figure 3.3. Scroll down the Styles list and select Template Tags.

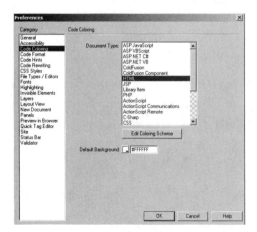
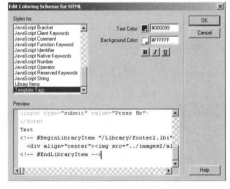

Figure 3.2   The Edit > Preferences dialog.   **Figure 3.3**   The Edit Color Scheme dialog.

You can change the style for the Template Tags by adding Bold, Italics, or Underline (as displayed in Code view window), and you can change the text and/or background color. The changes you make here apply only to the Template files themselves, not the child pages. There is no Reset Color Scheme button here, so we have listed them for your convenience. One last thing to note is that the Preview field is not a live display; it does not visually represent any changes you make.

The Code Coloring defaults are listed in Table 3.2.

Table 3.2   Code Coloring Defaults

Heading	Setting
Text Color	#000099
Background Color	#FFFFFF
Bold	Deselected
Italic	Deselected
Underline	Deselected

That is how it's supposed to work! We found during testing that these changes are not reflected in template or child pages, sadly, so you can ignore this setting for Template Tags presently. Hopefully this will be fixed in future releases of this product.

Highlighting Options

You can change the highlighting colors and visibility by choosing Edit > Preferences and choosing the Highlighting category (see Figure 3.4). This tab and the View menu work hand-in-hand.

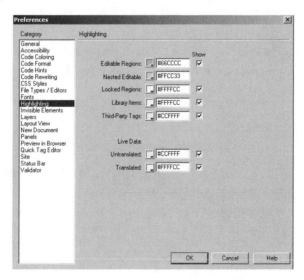

Figure 3.4   Edit > Preferences dialog, Highlighting Category selected.

As you can see in the figure, several options are available in this category. We are concerned with only three in relationship to templates. These are editable regions; Nested Editable; and Locked Regions. Note that these preferences affect only Design view displays and not Code view coloring. Each of these items is discussed in the following sections.

Editable Regions

This selection pair enables you to see editable areas defined in template files and carried through to child pages. By removing the checkmark in the Show field, you are disabling the editable region markings from appearing on the pages, thereby making it very difficult to locate where you can change content. The color is used as a highlight for the editable region name as well as an outline of the editable regions visible area in Design view. The defaults are #66CCCC and Show Checked.

Nested Editable

This preference allows you to select a color to use for displaying nested editable regions in nested templates, as well as child pages of the nested template. The default is #FFCC33.

Locked Regions

This selection pair enables you to see locked areas defined in template files and carried through to child pages. By removing the checkmark in the Show field, you are disabling the locked region markings from appearing on the pages, which you may decide is more visually appealing. The color is used as a highlight for the locked region name as well as an outline of the locked regions visible area in Design view. The defaults are #FFFFCC and Show Checked.

View Menu

Choose View > Visual Aids and make sure that Invisible Elements is checked and Hide All is not checked; otherwise, you will not be able to see the template regions on the page (see Figure 3.5). This view option is page-specific and not universal, which means that you might have to make adjustments for each document you open if you have previously changed it from its default.

Figure 3.5   Choosing View > Visual Aids to display invisible elements.

Region Naming Conventions

Please observe your OS-specific naming conventions. Be wary of JavaScript reserved words, and do not name the regions the same way you name layers or images. Each region name must be unique. For example, you can use a practical naming convention like r_name_of_region so that you can tell what is what when you edit the code by hand.

Templates the Old Way

In the "old days," templates were much simpler than they are now. Although the basic elements of templates (editable and non-editable regions) are the same in all versions of DW, DMX has added a great many new capabilities to the toolkit.

To understand these differences, let's first examine each as they were implemented in earlier versions of Dreamweaver. Methods for working with DW4 and earlier templates and template elements are described here briefly; more attention is devoted to those of DMX, however.

The Base Dreamweaver Template Code

The Dreamweaver/UltraDev 4 (Dreamweaver) template document has a document structure that is specific to templates. If you were to open Dreamweaver and create a new file, and then save it as a template named MyTest, you would have a document that was coded as you see here:

```
<html>
<head>
<!-- #BeginEditable "doctitle" -->
<title>Untitled Document</title>
<!-- #EndEditable -->
<meta http-equiv="Content-Type" content="text/html; charset=iso-8859-1">
</head>
<body bgcolor="#FFFFFF" text="#000000">
</body>
</html>
```

The starting, or blank, template has only one editable region—the doctitle region, which allows you to change the page title tag in child pages based on this template. This is a default and standard editable region when creating a template in Dreamweaver. The template engine overlooks it as an editable region, however, and when this template is saved, you will get a warning message advising that there are no editable regions on the page.

> **Note**
>
> There seems to have been a bug in Dreamweaver 4 that occasionally would leave out this editable region when a pre-made file was used to create a template document. This does cause a slight amount of grief until the issue is discovered, but the editable region can be added in Code view of the template and when saved, your child pages will have an editable title once you propagate the template changes to the child pages.

A child page created from this template would have the following document structure:

```
<html>
<!-- #BeginTemplate "/Templates/MyTest.dwt" -->
<head>
<!-- #BeginEditable "doctitle" -->
<title>Untitled Document</title>
<!-- #EndEditable -->
<meta http-equiv="Content-Type" content="text/html; charset=iso-8859-1">
</head>
<body bgcolor="#FFFFFF" text="#000000">
</body>
<!-- #EndTemplate -->
</html>
```

Because there is no `<body>`...`</body>` area editable regions, you get the same warning screen again.

Notice that all template-related markup (these are actually comments, but Dreamweaver interprets them as tags and we will call them *template markup*) in both the template and its children are all preceded by the # character. This is how Dreamweaver recognizes the comment tag as template-specific markup.

The child has one other specific template markup region that is unique to child pages. That's the second line:

```
<!-- #BeginTemplate "/Templates/MyTest.dwt" -->
```

This tells the child page which template is associated with it and also tells the template engine that this child page should be updated when the parent template is changed.

Now that you understand the basics of the template and child structure, we will explore the two region types available to Dreamweaver. If you're wondering where Dreamweaver MX structure fits in this discussion, it will be presented soon in the section entitled, "The Base Dreamweaver MX Code."

Non-Editable Regions

Non-editable regions constitute the "boilerplate" part of templates. This is the part of the template page that will be "protected" on each child page, and it's the part that gives all the child pages their "family" look. All the elements on the template page are inherited by all of that template's child pages at the moment the child pages are created. From that point forward, only changes to these non-editable regions of a parent template page will be propagated to child pages by DW/DMX. A single edit to a single template page's non-editable region could affect many child pages; hence, their utility and reliability.

Note

Dealing with template child pages is simple until you start to consider nested templates, covered later in this chapter. Be forewarned that we will have to augment our nomenclature for child pages to include some sense of generation; that is, a child of the topmost parent or of a child of the parent! Confused yet? See what we mean?

What Can Non-Editable Regions Contain?

Non-editable regions can contain any valid code, HTML, JavaScript, VBScript, and so on.

How Do You Recognize Non-Editable Regions?

When opening a template page, you can identify the non-editable regions only by negative inference. Looking for the editable regions in Code view or Design view will reveal which regions are editable, which means that you'll also be able tell which regions are *not* editable (that's negative inference, folks!).

When opening a child page, the non-editable regions are identifiable in Code view by the gray color of the code (as opposed to the straw highlighting in DW). Pointing at one of these same regions in Design view produces a "slashed circle" cursor. These regions are locked, and you can't make any changes in them at the child-page level.

How Do You Work with Non-Editable Regions?

Using DW/DMX, you can edit template pages freely, whether in editable or non-editable regions. As mentioned earlier, changes to non-editable regions are propagated when the template page is saved. Changes to editable regions are reflected only in new pages created from the template, but are not propagated to existing child pages of this template.

Obviously, edits to non-editable regions cannot be performed in child pages.

Editable Regions

An editable region is what allows each child of a given template page to contain unique code.

What Can Editable Regions Contain?

An editable region usually can be applied to (hence, contain) any valid page element, but some may produce unexpected results. Page elements are shown in Table 3.3 (this table is applicable to both DW and DMX).

Table 3.3   Page Elements and Their Suitability for Template Regions

Page Element	Comment
HEAD contents	DW must have Editable regions manually added to the HEAD of the document to allow for child page-specific content. Do this by opening the template page, displaying Code view, and typing the editable region tags. When you're finished, each child page will support unique content in this area, including Meta Tags, JavaScript, CSS, and so forth.
	DMX automatically creates the editable region for you when a new template file is created or a file is saved as a template. This editable region's name is HEAD.

Page Element	Comment
	To add **HEAD** content on a child page, select View > Head Content, select the cyan outlined icon on the Head Content toolbar, and use Insert > Head Tags to insert your **HEAD** data with ease.
Table `<table>`	A table contained in an editable region and its attributes are fully editable in child pages. In fact, the table can be deleted from the page because the entire table is wrapped in editable region tags.
Row `<tr>`	In DW, it is not possible to make an editable region containing multiple cells.
	If the table is a single-column table, it is possible to create an editable region after selecting a `<tr>` tag on the Quick Tag Selector. Although you can do this, DW correctly puts the editable region between the `<td>` tag pair (because content between `<tr>` and `<td>` is not allowed). However, doing this leaves the editable region tags empty, making it very hard to insert content in a child page.
	In DMX, a table row can be specified as an editable region. The advantage of this is that it can then act as an editable table, where you can add multiple rows to insert the content (see the discussion of repeat tables, in Chapter 2). The `<tr>` tags are wrapped in the editable region code as they should be. You cannot wrap a `<td>` in an editable region, however.
Cell `<td>`	An editable region is inserted within the cell. The region is "held open" with text content taken from the name of the region. If the region is named `TableContent`, the editable region's code will look like this:

DW:

```
<td><!-- #BeginEditable "TableContent" -->
{TableContent}<!-- #EndEditable --></td>
```

DMX:

```
<td><!-- TemplateBeginEditable
"TableContent" -->TableContent
<!-- TemplateEndEditable --></td>
```

Propping the editable region open like this makes it easy to add content in a child page.

Attributes of the containing cell tag will not be editable in child pages—that is, alignment, background images, or color—reflecting the fact that what is being made editable is the contents of the cell, not the cell's HTML attributes. Contrast this with the result of making a table editable.

Table 3.3   Continued

Page Element	Comment
Image `<img>`	The tag's attributes are made editable in child pages. This allows you to change all available attributes for such an image, including size, border, alignment, `vspace` and `hspace`, Alt Tag contents, and so on. In addition, an `<img>` tag within an editable region can be removed from the child page.
	It is not possible to add an image map to such an image—at least not through DW's UI. If you want to add an image map to an image that is part of a template page, create a dummy page, insert and map the image, and copy and paste the image and its associated map into the template page (a more complete procedure is detailed in Macromedia's *Technote #13880*, at `www.macromedia.com/go/13880`).
Plain text ("abc")	Functions as expected. Be aware that an inline editable text region (with text bare on the page, not contained in a table or a layer); for example,
	DW:
	`<body><!-- #BeginEditable "plain_text" -->` `abcd<!-- #EndEditable --></body>`
	DMX

	`<body><!-- TemplateBeginEditable`
	`"plain_text" -->abcd`
	`<!-- TemplateEndEditable --></body>`

	will not allow the insertion of a block-level element like a table or layer. (In DMX, such constructions display a warning that it will not be possible to insert other block-level tags.)
	In addition, you cannot add a block-level page element between `<font>` tags or any other in-line styling tags, such as `<b>`, `<i>`, `<u>`, and so on.
Hyperlink `<a href="#">Link</a>`	Functions as expected. The link's properties are fully editable, including URL, target, and all font properties.
Layer `<div>`	Functions as expected. The layer's contents and inline styles are fully editable, including positioning, clipping, and so on. If, however, only the content of the layer is an editable region, the layer cannot be repositioned, because it is not also editable by virtue of simply containing an editable region.
Form `<form>`	Functions as expected. The form and its contents are fully editable, including the form tag's attributes and contained form elements.
Flash element (`swf`)	All attributes are editable.

In DW, editable regions can contain other page elements, but not other editable regions, of course. In DMX, this… well, read on.

Adding a Layer to a Child Page

Have you ever had a problem adding a "layer" to a child page? Plenty of people who post to the DW newsgroup do, and here's a tip to help you with this common task: There are two problems with trying to add layers to template child pages, depending on how the layer is being added:

- If you are adding the layer using Insert > Layer, it is critically important to be aware of the positioning of your insertion point on the page—a carelessly inserted layer (that is, one that has been dropped into a table or another layer) can cause plenty of cross-browser problems with your page.

- Attempting to add a layer by using the Object Panel (clicking the Layer Object and dragging it onto the page—an inherently much safer way to add layers to a page because there is no risk of inadvertent nesting) is often unsuccessful because DW tries to write this code just below the <body> tag, and this area of a child page is usually locked.

Here are two ways to make it easy to add layers to child pages (and ones that avoid both of these problems).

The first is to build a "layer landing pad" at the bottom of the template. Here's how:

Open the template page and (in Code view) put this code

```
<p> </p >
```

immediately before the </body> tag. Make that an editable region called layerpad, for example. Saving the template page will put this editable region on each child page. In the child page, click this region and then use DW's Insert > Layer. This method will work well.

Alternatively, you can insert a layer safely in the template (give it a unique name, such as holding), leave it empty, and make the entire layer editable (the layer—not only its contents) by selecting the entire layer and choosing Insert > Template Objects > Editable region (which will wrap the layer inside the editable region). Give this editable region a unique name so that you can recognize it at a glance in the child page. You can then, in the child page, add layers by selecting the original layer's Visual Aid marker in Design view (the yellow anchor shield), pressing the right- or left-arrow key (which leaves your insertion point still within the original layer's editable region but outside the holding layer itself, thereby preventing nesting of layers), and selecting Insert > Layer.

Note

There may also be issues encountered when attempting to add an image map to an editable region in a template's child page. These issues and their solution are completely covered in Macromedia's excellent *Tech Note #13880*, which can be found by using this URL: www.macromedia.com/go/13880.

> **Note**
>
> DW template markup is completely editable in DMX; however, if you add any editable regions in DMX and then open the document in DW, the edit will not be usable. Templates are forward-compatible but not backward-compatible. General advice: Do not edit DMX templates in DW, period!

How Do You Recognize Editable Regions?

In DMX, Macromedia has changed the structure/syntax of the markup used to define editable and non-editable regions, most likely because of the expanded capabilities of templates. In DW4 and earlier, looking at Code or Design view of either a child or a parent template page can identify a template's editable regions. (DMX's syntax will be dealt with later in the "Templates the New Way" section of this chapter.)

In Code view of a template or child page, a DW editable region is defined by the presence of markup tags like these (see Figure 3.6):

```
<!-- #BeginEditable "sidebar" -->
...
<!-- #EndEditable -->
```

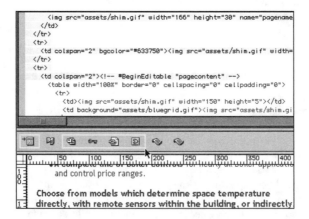

Figure 3.6   Code highlighting for editable regions. Note the manually added editable regions in the head (as shown by the cyan outline of the icons).

These are ordinary HTML comments, but they are ones that are critically important to DW's templates. The function of these comments is apparent from the information within the tag: The former defines the beginning of an editable region called `sidebar`, and the latter is generic for the end of any editable region. Any content within these two tags will be specific to the page on which it appears; that is, there is no inheritance of this code between child and parent pages.

When examining this page in Design view, you can identify editable regions (in both template and child) in a different way. According to DW's Preferences settings, template editable regions (and library items) could have any color, but the default for DW is to outline such areas with a cyan color and to identify them with the region's name in a cyan-colored tab.

It may happen that these editable region tabs cover other important information on the Design view page. In this event, you can hide all these visual aids by pressing Ctrl+Shift+I or select View > Visual Aids > Hide All. Now you will be able to see the underlying content.

How Do You Work with Editable Regions?

In a template, editable regions can be added, deleted, and modified, at will.

To add an editable region, select or click within the desired page element (refer back to Table 3.3), and choose Modify > Templates > New Editable Region. To remove an editable region, choose Modify > Templates > Remove Editable Region. The content of an editable region can be modified as usual, but these changes will not be propagated to existing child pages. You can select an editable region either by clicking on the name tab in Design view (see Figure 3.7), or by selecting the <mm:editable> tag shown on the Tag Selector region of the DW document window's status bar (see Figure 3.8). Selecting an editable region by using either of these two methods, and pressing the Delete key, also will delete the editable region and its contents.

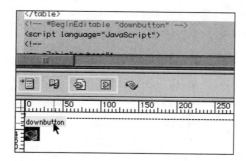

Figure 3.7   Using the editable region's name tab to select the entire region (including the defining comment tags—see Code view).

In a child page, editable regions are freely editable (this is subject to the sidebar following Table 3.3 about inserting a layer into a table) but they cannot be selected, added, or deleted. Any content within an editable region is completely safe and will not be overwritten by automatic updates of the template page. A given page may contain any number of editable regions.

Figure 3.8   Using the quick tag selector to select an editable region (just after clicking `<mm:editable>`).

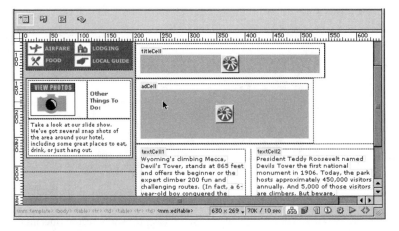

Figure 3.9   Four separate editable regions are found on this page.

Templates the New Way

Because the scope of DMX's templates has been significantly expanded, it has been necessary to change the method of identifying template editable regions, as well as of invoking other new capabilities of templates.

In order to do this, Macromedia has created five new types of regions, as well as some new template "wrinkles." This section examines and describes each of these. Later sections elaborate on these descriptions and provide examples of their use.

The Base Dreamweaver MX Template Code

The Dreamweaver MX (DMX) template document has a document structure that, when created, is specific to templates. If you were to open DMX, create a new file using File > New > General Tab > Basic Page, select HTML Template, and save it as MyTest, you would have a document that was coded as follows:

```
<!DOCTYPE HTML PUBLIC "-//W3C//DTD HTML 4.01 Transitional//EN">
<html>
<head>
<!-- TemplateBeginEditable name="doctitle" -->
<title>Untitled Document</title>
<!-- TemplateEndEditable -->
<meta http-equiv="Content-Type" content="text/html; charset=iso-8859-1">
<!-- TemplateBeginEditable name="head" -->
<!-- TemplateEndEditable -->
</head>
<body>
</body>
</html>
```

You may notice at first glance that there are several differences between this blank template and a blank Dreamweaver 4 template. These differences are discussed next.

The first difference is that the DMX template has a DOCTYPE declaration (this was a high-volume request by previous Dreamweaver users). The template now has two default editable regions: the doctitle and head regions. The doctitle region serves the same purpose mentioned earlier in the section, "The Base Dreamweaver Template Code." The head region is where you can put page-specific information such as custom JavaScript, meta tags, and page-specific CSS (this also was a high-volume request by previous Dreamweaver users and could be added only by hand previously in Dreamweaver). The last difference we want to point out is that DMX does not use the # character to point out template-specific markup to the template engine any longer. (Please see earlier comments about template pages containing *only* editable document title regions.)

A child page that is created from this template would have a document structure as you see in the following code:

```
<!DOCTYPE HTML PUBLIC "-//W3C//DTD HTML 4.01 Transitional//EN">
<html><!-- InstanceBegin template="/Templates/MyTest.dwt"
codeOutsideHTMLIsLocked="false" -->
<head>
```

```
<!-- InstanceBeginEditable name="doctitle" -->
<title>Untitled Document</title>
<!-- InstanceEndEditable -->
<meta http-equiv="Content-Type" content="text/html; charset=iso-8859-1">
<!-- InstanceBeginEditable name="head" -->
<!-- InstanceEndEditable -->
</head>
<body>
</body>
<!-- InstanceEnd --></html>
```

Because there is no <body>...</body> area editable regions, you get the same nag screen as mentioned earlier.

You may have noticed that the DMX and Dreamweaver child pages have several differences. Again, the DMX template does not use the # character to identify template markup. The template markup has changed from `TemplateBeginEditable` to `InstanceBeginEditable` (the change also applies to the region closing tags). It should be obvious to you that the template engine has matured and become much more sophisticated!

The child has one other specific template markup that is unique to child pages. That's the second line identified as

```
<!-- InstanceBegin template="/Templates/MyTest.dwt"
codeOutsideHTMLIsLocked="false" -->
```

This tells the child page which template is associated with it and also tells the template engine that this child page should be updated when the parent template is changed. The last parameter of this markup `codeOutsideHTMLIsLocked="false"` is discussed later in the section, "Editing Code Outside of HTML Tags."

Note

DMX will recognize and use Dreamweaver template markup without incident. What this means is that Dreamweaver 4 templates can be opened, modified, and changed in DMX and all regions will remain intact.

Warning

After a Dreamweaver 4 template has been modified by DMX, do not make any further edits to the template in Dreamweaver 4 or data corruption may occur, due to template schema differences.

Now that you know the basics of the DMX template and child structure, you can explore the many region types available to DMX.

DMX Non-Editable Regions

What can we say? A non-editable region is a part of the page that is simply not editable. This is the same in DMX as in DW. You can't edit this code at all in a child page.

DMX Editable Regions

DMX's editable regions are functionally the same as DW's editable regions, except in two regards:

- The syntax of the identifying comment tags that wrap them
- The method of applying an editable region to the page

Examining an editable region in DW's Code view (for either a template or a child page) reveals this familiar code:

```
<!-- #BeginEditable "sidebar" -->
...
<!-- #EndEditable -->
```

The same editable region as written in DMX is defined this way in a template file:

```
<!-- TemplateBeginEditable name="sidebar" -->
...
<!-- TemplateEndEditable -->
```

and this way in a child page:

```
<!-- InstanceBeginEditable name="sidebar" -->
...
<!-- InstanceEndEditable -->
```

Editable regions can be inserted in Design or Code view and can be inserted at the current cursor position or will wrap the currently selected content.

When an editable region is selected (or clicked), the Tag Selector displays `<mmtemplate: editable>` for a template page and `<mmtinstance:editable>` for a child page.

In DW, you apply an editable region by using Modify > Templates > New Editable Region.

In DMX, an editable region is applied either by using Insert > Template Objects > Editable Region or by clicking the editable region's icon in the Insert panel's Templates tab or by right-clicking to display the context menu and selecting Templates > New Editable Region (see Figure 3.11).

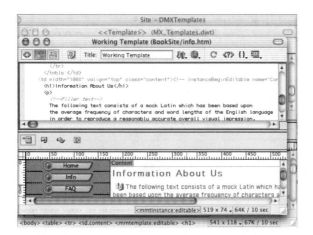

Figure 3.10   Superimposed template and child pages, showing Quick Tag Selector differences.

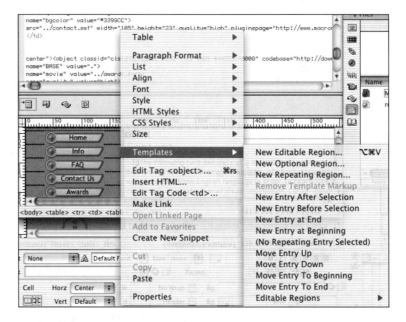

Figure 3.11   The Templates context menu displayed by Command+clicking on the Mac or by right-clicking on the PC.

In all other regards, DW and DMX handle and display editable regions in an equivalent fashion. In addition, the comments in Table 3.3 apply also to editable regions in DMX.

In addition to these two familiar regions, the wizards at Macromedia have devised five new regions to enhance and extend DMX's templates: repeating regions, repeating tables, optional regions, editable optional regions, and MultipleIF conditional regions.

The Template Program

A template is like a little program for generating an HTML page. In DW, this program was very simple. All it did was place the locked HTML from the template page into the child page, with no modifications, at the time that the child page was spawned or the template page was saved after changes (that is, these two instances are the only times that the program runs). The only differences between each of the individual child pages was the contents of the editable regions.

In Dreamweaver MX, the template program is *much* more complicated. In addition to adding another call to the template program (in DMX, it now also runs any time a template parameter is changed in a child page), many new elements have been added to the template envelope, allowing template pages actually to operate using logical tests on its content. Thus, a template now can conditionally include content in a page using conditional regions, which are examined in the page by the template program as the page is being updated. Then the template can output different HTML code for each page. The behavior of conditional regions is determined either by template parameters on the page or the result of evaluating a template expression.

Template Parameters

The template program is run whenever a child page is created, updated, or saved. As with all programs, there must be some kind of data input into the program; otherwise, it would just produce the same results every time it's run! In the case of templates, the input takes the form of template parameters.

Template parameters are pieces of data that may have a different value in each instance of a template. For example, in the toy store site, you might define a product section using a template. Each page within this section would represent one product in the store. Each product would have a name and a section, which would be unique for that product. The name and the section values could each be a template parameter for that page.

Each template parameter has a name, a data type, and a default value (used to fill in the initial value of the parameter when a new instance is created, or when a new parameter is defined and existing instances are updated). Template parameters are defined using a tag in the head section of the template document. A template parameter definition tag looks like this (a snippet for producing one of these has been included in the extension provided on the book site):

```
<!-- TemplateParam name="section" type="text" value="" -->
```

Template parameter tags can be inserted only into template pages themselves and not in the child pages. A similar tag you will see later in this section can be inserted into the child pages, and it contains the value of the parameter for that page.

You must have the name, type, and value attributes in your parameter tags. If you don't supply a default value, DMX will supply it for you by entering either the empty string, 0, or false, depending on whether the type is text, numeric, or boolean, respectively. In this case, the tag defines a parameter named section whose type is text (that is, any text string is a valid value for this parameter), and whose default value is the empty string. If you are wondering how to get the definition tag into the template page, be patient and read on!

A template parameter can be one of the following types:

- **boolean**—In this case, the default value, and the value in the instances, must either be true or false.

- **number**—The value must be a number. The format used is IEEE 64-bit floating point, and any number that can fit in a 64-bit floating point variable is legal (positive, negative, and decimals).

- **text**—The value can be any text string. You can entity encode the string, just as you would with any HTML attribute value—any string that can be stored in an HTML tag attribute is legal as a value here. An example of an encoded string might be "Quoted Text Example".

- **color**—The value is an HTML color, either the standard named colors, like red or magenta, or an expression of the form #XXXXXX like #FF00FF. You can also use a shorthand html color like #09C.

- **URL**—A path/filename to be used on the page. The rules governing what can be entered here are identical to those for any other URL on your page.

Note

It would be wise to be very cautious with URL parameters in template pages, and make sure that they get properly updated when the target file is moved or renamed.

A parameter's name must follow the same rules as for repeated region names and must not conflict with the name of another parameter in the same template, although it may take the same name as that of another repeated region or editable region. (Although we are hard pressed to imagine why you would want to do this!) Parameter names are case-sensitive.

Note that for each parameter defined in the template file, there will be a corresponding *instance parameter tag* appearing in the child page. The instance parameter tag stores the value of the parameter for that particular child page. In this example, the instance parameter tag might look like this:

```
<!-- InstanceParam name="section" type="text" value="preschool" -->
```

This code directs that the parameter named `section` has the value `preschool` in this page. In another page, this same parameter could have a different value, such as `elementaryschool`. You will use these extensively in building the Hot Cool Toys site.

Creating Template Parameters in the Template File

You have two ways to create a template parameter in the template file. The first is to create an optional region and enter the name of the parameter as the name of the region. This automatically creates a template parameter in the `head` section of the file and uses the parameter to control the optional region.

The other way to create a template parameter is to directly type in the parameter definition tag, in the `<head>...</head>` area of the document using Code view, or to insert the template parameter snippet. Again, you use this method during the project chapters.

Note

There is no way provided in DMX to create a template parameter using the Design view.

Template Expressions

Note

Please be aware that the syntax shown in the DMX Help files regarding template expressions is sometimes erroneous. The syntax shown in this document is correct, and should be used rather than that currently shown in DMX (the initial retail release version).

This section looks at how DMX has made the template program for updating the child page even more flexible and sophisticated by using a mechanism called *template expressions.*

An expression is a little bit of JavaScript-like programming logic (`a==b` or `name!='foo'`) used to make a decision about some content in the template instance, which can be included in the template's child page. It provides a way to use, combine, and output template parameters and other properties in each template instance or child page.

Template expressions can be used to insert HTML in places that are either too "small" to use a whole template region (such as a tag attribute) or places that need to change in each child page, but are not intended to be editable directly through Design view. For example, the name of the section for a product might appear in several places in the page. Rather than leaving it to the page author to enter it in each place (and possibly overlooking it or entering incorrectly), we can use a template expression to allow it to be entered only once. Template expressions also can be used instead of a simple condition inside conditional template regions to produce more complex conditional inclusion of content in the template instance.

You can enter a template expression into a page by entering it in a comment line, as shown here:

```
<!-- TemplateExpr expr="section" -->
```

This is a *template expression tag.* (Well, it's really a comment, but, as in DW, it's a comment that pretends to be a tag, complete with attributes.) This tells the template program to generate some HTML here using that template expression. The expression is just the string inside the `expr` attribute of the tag.

In this case, the entire expression is just the `section` parameter, which tells the template engine to "evaluate the value of the parameter named `section` and output it into the template instance." Child pages of this template will display the product's section here. You can use any formatting around this expression to make the section line look the way you want it to.

An Alternate Expression Syntax

Sometimes you may want to use a template expression in a place where it is syntactically impossible or impractical to use an HTML comment. For example, you might want to use a template expression inside the `bgColor` attribute of the `<body>` tag to control the background color of some of your pages by generating the color differently for each child page. In this case, there is another syntax you can use that is equivalent to the template expression tag. This is called the @@ syntax.

The @@ syntax looks like this:

@@(expr)@@

The expr can be the same as the expression in the tag syntax shown earlier. The preceding example would look like this in the @@ syntax:

@@(section)@@

You can place this almost anywhere in a document, in the main flow, just like a comment or tag, or inside a tag attribute, like this:

<a href="@@(link)@@">my link</A>

It can even be placed inside a tag, but outside any of the attributes, in order to dynamically generate some of the tag attributes:

<a @@(customAttributes)@@>my other link</a>

When you use the @@ syntax, DMX creates an icon in Design view that can be selected to allow you to edit the expression in a Property Inspector. The icons look as shown in Figure 3.12.

Figure 3.12   The Design view expression symbol.

More Complex Template Expressions

All template expressions are written using the template language. This language is a small subset of JavaScript and uses JavaScript syntax and precedence rules. This code is run whenever a child of the template is created, updated, or saved.

Note that this is just a subset of JavaScript, and it's mostly meant to allow you to do comparisons, and so on. It doesn't let you do any of the things you typically do when programming, like define variables and functions, use regular expressions, modify strings, and more.

The following features of JavaScript are supported:

- **numeric literals, string literals, boolean literals** (`true or false`)—This means that you can use these values in your expressions. For example, if we wanted to have an optional region that appeared only on pages in the `'preschool'` section of the site, we could set it up by comparing the `'section'` parameter with the string literal 'preschool':

```
<!-- TemplateBeginIf cond="section=='preschool'" -->
Hey!
Just for Preschool!
<!-- TemplateEndIf -->
```

  Note that in the case of a string literal, because the expression is going to appear inside a tag attribute, you have to be a little careful about how you handle the quotation marks around the string literal. In this case, we've used single quotes, so they nest correctly. If, for some reason, you want to use double quotes, you can do it by entity encoding them in the expression—DMX will decode the expression before evaluating it. Here's an example where Dreamweaver encodes the quotes in the expression `section == "preschool"` so that it could be placed inside the tag attribute of the optional region. DMX changed the character " to the encoded form: "

```
<!-- TemplateBeginIf cond="section=='&quot;preschool&quot;'" -->
Hey!
Just for Preschool!
<!-- TemplateEndIf -->
```

- **variable reference**— There are two predefined variables that can be used by expressions that are inside a repeating region. DMX uses the standard JavaScript syntax for referencing these variables. An example and description of these variables is given in the later list, "Expression Objects."

- **field reference**—DMX can reference fields of a variable using the `'dot'` syntax, familiar from JavaScript. This is used only inside a repeating region to access fields of the current repeat object. An example of this is given in the code following the list "Expression Objects," later in this chapter.

- **unary operators**—These are the standard operators:

Operator	Description
+	Plus (for incrementing a number)
−	Minus (for decrementing a number)
~	XOR (for number values)
!	NOT (negate a boolean value)

- **binary operators**—Again, the standard binary operators are supported:

Operator	Description
+	Plus (arithmetic)
−	Minus (arithmetic)
×	Multiply (arithmetic)
/	Divide (arithmetic)
%	Modulus
&	Bitwise AND (for number fields)
|	Bitwise OR
&&	Boolean AND (compares boolean values)
||	Boolean OR
<	Less than
<=	Less than or equal to
>	Greater than
>=	Greater than or equal to
==	Equal to (comparison)
!=	Not equal to (comparison)
=	Equal(assignment)
<<	Bit Shift Left (used for integers to shift the pattern of bits to the direction specified)
>>	Bit Shift Right

- **conditional operator**—DMX supports the standard JavaScript conditional operator: ?: So, a user may write an expression of the form:

```
@@(section=='preschool' ? <B> : <I>)@@
```

This operator evaluates the expression on the left, and, if true, outputs the HTML between the ? and the :; otherwise, it outputs what's after the :. So, in this case, if section stores the value 'preschool', this will output a <B> tag; otherwise it will output an <I> tag.

- **parentheses**—You can use parentheses to control the scope of evaluation in a conditional, to group operands, or to just make the code more readable. An example would be a more complex expression in the preceding page:

```
<!-- TemplateBeginIf cond="(section=='preschool') && (toyName=='Elmo' ||
toyName=='Bert')" -->
Hey!
Just for Preschool! It's @@(toyName)@@
<!-- TemplateEndIf -->
```

The only objects available are those defined by the Expression Object Model.

DMX is a bit different from standard JavaScript in terms of errors and type conversions. For example, referencing an undefined field is an error. DMX does not support the JavaScript `null` or `undefined` types, so if you save a file or check syntax on it, you will get a syntax error if you use this type.

All objects support "method call syntax" for a single method, named `_Get`. This is used to access fields whose names contain spaces, punctuation, or other characters that are not part of a valid JavaScript identifier, or whose name conflicts with a JavaScript keyword. For example, `_document._Get("section")` is equivalent to `_document.section`, while `_document._Get("secondary title")` can be used to access a parameter named `"secondary title"`, which can't be accessed using field syntax.

Just remember that if you have a parameter with a space in its name, you'll need to use `_Get` when referring to it in an expression. In addition, you must use the `_Get` method to access any property whose name conflicts with a JavaScript keyword.

JavaScript Keywords

JavaScript keywords are `abstract`, `boolean`, `byte`, `break`, `case`, `catch`, `char`, `class`, `const`, `continue`, `debugger`, `default`, `delete`, `do`, `double`, `else`, `enum`, `export`, `extends`, `false`, `final`, `finally`, `float`, `for`, `function`, `goto`, `if`, `implements`, `import`, `in`, `instanceof`, `int`, `interface`, `long`, `native`, `new`, `null`, `package`, `private`, `protected`, `public`, `return`, `short`, `static`, `super`, `switch`, `synchronized`, `this`, `throw`, `throws`, `transient`, `true`, `try`, `typeof`, `var`, `volatile`, `void`, `while`, and `with`.

Most people will never have to worry about this. If you want, you can simply stick with the `_Get` method, and not think about this. But if you inadvertently use one of the preceding words as a parameter name and you get a syntax error from DMX, just remember that you can either change the name of the parameter or use the `_Get` method, and you'll be fine.

In addition to the basic syntax, an expression also can make reference to some standard objects. The following objects are defined by Dreamweaver MX where appropriate (the material in the following list is taken from DMX's Help text, and expanded or clarified where needed).

Expression Objects:

- `repeat`.   This variable is only defined for expressions appearing inside a repeated region and provides built-in information about the region:

  - `_index`. This is the numerical index of the entry containing the expression. The index of the first entry is 0.

  - `_numRows`. This is the total number of entries in this repeated region.

  - `_isFirst`.   This is true if the current entry is the first entry in its repeated region.

  - `_isLast`. This is true if the current entry is the last entry in its repeated region.

  - `_prevRecord`. The `_repeat` object for the previous entry. You will get an error when this property is accessed for the first entry in the region.

  - `_nextRecord`. The `_repeat` object for the next entry. You will get an error when this property is accessed for the last entry in the region.

  - `_parent`. The `_repeat` object for the enclosing repeated region. You will get an error if you access this property when the repeated region is not enclosed in another repeated region.

- `_document`. This contains the document-level template data. It has a field for each defined parameter in the template.

These variables are also accessible implicitly. For example, instead of saying `_document.section` in our first example, to get at the `'section'` parameter, we just said `'section'`, and DMX assumed the _document part. This is also true for the _repeat variable, when an expression is inside a `repeat` region.

The one main exception to this is nested repeated regions. When an expression is evaluated inside the inner repeated region, only fields of the innermost repeated region are available implicitly. Outer regions must be explicitly referenced using `_parent`.

Let's have an example of this. Make a new page and insert a table into it. Select the first row, and make it into a repeating region. The table should look like this:

```
<table width="75%" border="1">
<!-- TemplateBeginRepeat name="RepeatRegion1" -->
<tr>
<td> </td>
<td> </td>
<td> </td>
</tr>
<!-- TemplateEndRepeat -->
</table>
```

Working in Code view, enter the following attribute into the TR tag:

```
bgColor="@@(_repeat._index%2 ? '#FF0000' : '#00FF00')@@"
```

so the table looks like this:

```
<table width="75%" border="1">
<!-- TemplateBeginRepeat name="RepeatRegion1" -->
<tr bgColor="@@(_repeat._index%2 ? '#FF0000' : '#00FF00')@@>
<td> </td>
<td> </td>
<td> </td>
</tr>
<!-- TemplateEndRepeat -->
</table>
```

What does this expression do? Let's take it in parts. First, the expression is inside the bgColor attribute. This means that it's going to output some HTML into this attribute in all the child pages. Because the TR tag is inside a repeating region, however, this expression will get 'run' for each entry in the repeat region, and it will be told the index of that entry when it is run. How is it told the index of the entry? That's what the fragment _repeat._index is for: It translates into the index of the current repeat entry. Using % 2 means to compute the value modulus 2—that is, compute the remainder after dividing by 2, so that if the number is odd, the remainder is 1, and if it's even, the remainder is 0.

Note

In fact, the remainder of this calculation is 0.5, but in modulo arithmetic, the remainder is rounded to the next integer value, which is 1.

Next, all this is inside the ?: operator, which means that 1 is evaluated as true and 0 is evaluated as false, so if the index of the entry is odd (modulus is 1) we will output #FF0000; otherwise, if the index is even, we will output ##00FF00. Create a child page and make some entries in the repeat region, and see what happens. You should see this in Figure 3.13.

Note

Like library items, template expressions also can be nested. In fact, we have used this approach in building the pages for the Hot Cool Toys site (see Chapter 6, "Building the Template"). Also like library items, we are uncertain about the depth to which these items can be nested; however, informal testing has shown no problems with nestings two deep, and none would be expected with those three deep.

Now that you have a good understanding of the details of template parameters and template expressions, you will have a much easier time following the conditional regions discussion.

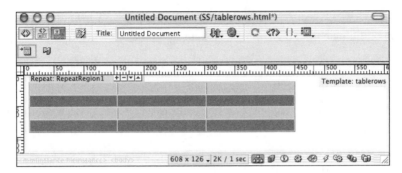

Figure 3.13   Table colors alternating in a repeating region using Design view.

Repeating Regions

A DMX repeating region defines a region of the page that can be optionally repeated multiple times on each child page, as with page-specific lists or images.

Once placed on the page, a repeat region must be edited manually if you want to change its name or its scope of action. In other words, there is no user interface for the region, other than the one invoked at the time it is inserted into the page.

You can insert repeating regions in Design or Code view. Additionally, you can insert the regions at the current cursor position or they will wrap the currently selected content. By default, repeating regions do not contain an editable region!

What Can Repeating Regions Contain?

A repeat region can contain (or be applied to) any valid HTML page element (refer to Table 3.3), as well as other DMX template regions (including editable regions, repeat tables, and so on). By themselves, repeat regions are not editable on child pages, but adding an editable region to one would provide this editability. Repeat regions could contain *other* repeat regions, allowing you to nest such effects in child pages. If repeat regions are nested, each such nested region can be manipulated independently.

How Do You Recognize Repeat Regions?

Repeat regions are identified differently in template and child pages.

In a template page, you can identify repeat regions in Code view by finding something similar to the following code:

```
<!-- TemplateBeginRepeat name="someRegionName" -->
RepeatRegioncontents
<!-- TemplateEndRepeat -->
```

In Design view, a repeat region is identified in a manner similar to an editable region, with an outlining border containing a tab and the name of the region.

When a repeat region is selected (or clicked), the Tag Selector displays:

```
<mmtemplate:repeat>
```

In a child page, repeat regions can be identified in Code view with this kind of designation:

```
<!-- InstanceBeginRepeat name="someRepeatRegionName" -->
RepeatRegioncontents
<!-- InstanceEndRepeatEntry -->
```

For each occurrence of multiple instances of a single repeat region, the preceding code will be modified by adding this:

```
<!-- InstanceBeginRepeatEntry -->
<!-- InstanceBeginEditable name="someEditRegion3" -->
RepeatRegion1
<!-- InstanceEndEditable -->
<!-- InstanceEndRepeatEntry -->
```

within the code for the repeat region when the repeat region also contains an editable region, and adding this

```
<!-- InstanceBeginRepeatEntry -->
RepeatRegion2
<!-- InstanceEndRepeatEntry -->
```

when it does not.

When you look at these regions in Design view, template pages and child pages will look identical (see Figure 3.14).

The code differences between template and child pages for repeat regions also is reflected in the designation used on the Tag Selector, where for a child page, the Tag Selector will show `<mmtinstance:repeat>`.

How Do You Work with Repeat Regions?

In a template page, you add a repeat region by selecting or clicking in an appropriate page element (refer to Table 3.3) and doing one of the following:

- Selecting Insert > Template Objects > Repeating Region
- Clicking the Repeating Region icon in the Insert Panel's Templates Tab
- Displaying the context menu and selecting Templates > New Repeating Region

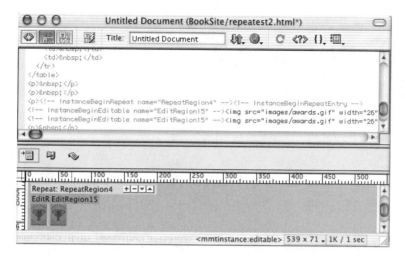

Figure 3.14   A repeat region containing an editable region. Note the Code view appearance and the Mini-user interface added to the repeat region.

To delete a repeat region, select the entire region by doing one of the following:

- Clicking the region name tab in Design view
- Selecting the `<mmtemplate:repeat>` tag on the Tag Selector
- Manually selecting the entire region's code in Code view and pressing the Delete key

Clicking within a repeat region reveals an `<mmtemplate:repeat>` tag on the Tag Selector. Selecting this tag or the repeat region's border tab will select the region, its contents, and its identifying comment tags. This means that selecting the tab and pressing the Delete key can delete a repeat region, removing the Region *and* its contents. On the other hand, a repeat region can be deleted by selecting the region and applying Modify > Templates > Remove Template Markup, which will remove the "wrapping" comment lines, but not the region's contents. (Remove Template Markup is explored extensively in Chapter 4.)

In a child page, repeat regions can be neither added nor deleted, but you can modify them by electing to repeat them none, one, or more times, or to reorder them on the page, if repeated.

To facilitate working with this and other of these new repeat regions in child pages, DMX attaches a Mini-User Interface (MUI) (refer to Figure 3.14) to the regions while editing a child page in Design view, allowing multiple instances of the repeat region to be inserted, deleted, or reordered. The functions offered by the MUI are also provided in several of DMX's standard menu options; that is, Edit > Repeating Entries Cut/Delete Repeating Entry or Modify > Templates > Repeating Entries > New Entry After Selection, New Entry Before Selection, New Entry at End, and New Entry at Beginning. In addition, you can move repeat regions with Modify > Templates > Repeating Entries > Move > Up, Down, To Beginning, and To End (refer to Figure 3.11).

You can also display the context menu and choose Templates. (We believe this is the best choice because 95 percent of the options for repeating regions are in this menu and easily accessible with a right-click (Control+Click).)

This MUI facilitates building page-specific, multiple instances of whatever contents are found within the repeat region. Simply clicking the + or – buttons permits the addition or deletion of the associated repeat region. In addition, you can change the order of multiple instances of a repeat region by using the up- and down-arrows in the MUI.

Because repeat regions will contain only editable regions that you might have placed, it is important to note that the MUI will produce slightly differing results when used in non-editable and editable repeat regions.

If a repeat region does not contain an editable region, its MUI will permit that repeat region only to be repeated, not deleted. In addition, once a repeat region has been repeated one or more times, you have no way to then change your mind to delete any of these instances of repetition. Finally, because the repeat region does not contain an editable region, there is no way to select the region's contents so that they can be reordered!

If a repeat region does contain an editable region, then it is possible to show that repeat region zero, one, or more times on the child page (showing zero times would require deleting the default instance of the repeat region's editable region by using the MUI or selecting the `<mmtinstance:editable>` tag on the Tag Selector and pressing Delete.

Repeating Tables

A DMX repeating table is a convenient way to add *both* a repeating region and an editable region in a single stroke. Because repeating regions are not, by default, also editable regions, using this template entity can be a timesaver in setting up a template page.

You can insert repeating tables in block mode only using Design or Code view. If there is something currently selected, this region type is inserted immediately after the current selection.

Fear not, there is a pseudo work-around! Add your table to the template, select a row, and insert a repeating region. Then for each cell on the horizontal axis, insert an editable region. You now have a repeating table in your template. Granted, there are a lot of mouse clicks involved, but if you have the need to wrap content, this is the only resolution presently available to you.

What Can Repeating Tables Contain?

In this specific instance, the options for what repeating tables can contain are restricted by the very nature of the tool. Inserting a repeating table will cause a table to be inserted within a repeat region. Any HTML page element that can safely be contained in a table, can therefore be contained in a repeating table.

How Do You Recognize Repeating Tables?

In both templates and child pages, repeat tables are identified similarly to repeat regions, with the following additions:

- They contain a table.
- Each cell (in the specified row) of this table is (by initial default) an editable region.

Examples of the resulting code are shown here:

In a template:

```
<table width="75%" border="3" cellspacing="0" cellpadding="0">
<!-- TemplateBeginRepeat name="RegionTable" -->
      <tr>
         <td><!-- TemplateBeginEditable name="EditRegion5" -->
          <!-- TemplateEndEditable --></td>
         <td><!-- TemplateBeginEditable name="EditRegion6" -->
          <!-- TemplateEndEditable --></td>
         <td><!-- TemplateBeginEditable name="EditRegion7" -->
          <!-- TemplateEndEditable --></td>
      </tr>
      <tr>
         <td><!-- TemplateBeginEditable name="EditRegion8" -->
          <!-- TemplateEndEditable --></td>
         <td><!-- TemplateBeginEditable name="EditRegion9" -->
          <!-- TemplateEndEditable --></td>
```

```
        <td><!-- TemplateBeginEditable name="EditRegion10" -->
         <!-- TemplateEndEditable --></td>
    </tr>
    <!-- TemplateEndRepeat -->
    <tr>
        <td> </td>
        <td> </td>
        <td> </td>
    </tr>
</table>
```

In a child page:

```
<table width="75%" border="3" cellspacing="0" cellpadding="0">
        <!-- InstanceBeginRepeat name="RepeatRegion9" -->
        <!-- InstanceBeginRepeatEntry -->
        <tr>
        <td><!-- InstanceBeginEditable name="EditRegion5" -->
         <!-- InstanceEndEditable --></td>
        <td><!— InstanceBeginEditable name="EditRegion6" -->
         <!-- InstanceEndEditable --></td>
        <td><!— InstanceBeginEditable name="EditRegion7" -->
         <!-- InstanceEndEditable --></td>
    </tr>
    <tr>
        <td><!-- InstanceBeginEditable name="EditRegion8" -->
         <!-- InstanceEndEditable --></td>
        <td><!-- InstanceBeginEditable name="EditRegion9" -->
         <!-- InstanceEndEditable --></td>
        <td><!-- InstanceBeginEditable name="EditRegion10" -->
         <!-- InstanceEndEditable --></td>
    </tr>
    <!-- InstanceEndRepeatEntry --><!-- InstanceEndRepeat -->
    <tr>
        <td> </td>
        <td> </td>
        <td> </td>
    </tr>
</table>
```

Note that true to its name, the repeat table is built *within* a table (and not around one), and that it is not necessary for all the cells and rows of the table to be editable, although when inserted, the selected row contains cells, each of which contains an editable region.

How Do You Work with Repeating Tables?

Working with a repeating table is nearly identical to working with a repeat region. Each has an MUI so that elements can be added, deleted, or reordered. The only real difference is that repeat regions might not also contain editable regions (you might not have inserted one), and repeat tables will always contain editable regions.

To insert a repeat table, position the cursor at the desired location in the template page, and choose one of the following:

- Insert > Template Objects > Repeating Table
- Click the repeating table icon on the Templates toolbar

Note

Curiously, there is no context menu option to insert a repeat table, so these two methods are the only ones available.

To delete a repeat table, select it in the template page by doing one of the following:

- Clicking the name tab in Design view
- Clicking the <mmtemplate:repeat> tag on the Quick Tag Selector, and pressing the Delete key

Note

Using the Quick Tag Selector method for selecting a repeat table that contains only a single repeat row may be confusing. When you select the <mmtemplate:repeat> tag by clicking it, the display immediately changes to show the selected <tr> tag, and the <mmtemplate:repeat> tag is deselected (and resists all further attempts to select it). In a multiple repeating row repeat table, this is not a problem.

Note

The editable region names that are inserted have no UI during the insertion of the repeating table, so you can manually change them using Code view or the Tag Selector. The Property inspector should populate with the appropriate inspector so you can change the default to the one you want.

Conditional Regions

Extending the concept of repeat regions, the next two new region types add the ability to associate their display with some logical determinant: either a parameter defined elsewhere on the page, or an expression that is evaluated at the time that the child page is saved within DMX. We will make substantial use of these regions and demonstrate how to apply these logical determinants while constructing the Hot Cool Toys template beginning in Chapter 6.

Conditional regions are made "optional" by way of the special template variables we have been discussing that are inserted by DMX when the regions are created on the template page. These variables take the form of template parameters, which DMX writes in an editable region in the <HEAD> of the document, and as a result, they are accessible in each child page. This allows each child page to control the value of these parameters independently, hence the display of the conditional region in each child page can be customized for that page.

DMX can create two special conditional regions—optional regions, and MultipleIf optional regions. The details of each are described in the following sections.

Optional Regions

Optional regions are an exciting new region type and part of what could be thought of as the conditional region group. An optional region added to the template page will be visible on the child pages depending on the value of its associated parameter.

You can insert optional regions in Design or Code view, either at the current cursor position or by wrapping the currently selected content. By default, optional regions do not contain an editable region!

Modifying a Parameter's Value

You control the value of a template parameter on each child page by using Modify > Template Properties. This is an important addition to the template envelope developed by Macromedia in DMX. By using Modify > Template Properties, it is possible to establish uniquely the value of every optional region's parameters on the page (more about this in later discussions).

The easiest way to do this is to use the Template Properties dialog. This dialog lets you set the values of template parameters in the child pages. Let's create a child page of the toy page template we created earlier by selecting the template in the Template panel and choosing New From Template from the context menu. With this child page open, select the menu item Modify > Template Properties. You'll see a dialog that looks like the one shown in Figure 3.15.

The figure shows the available parameters for this child page in the left column of the list and the current values, if any, in the right. If you click one of the parameter names, a set of controls appears at the bottom of the dialog to allow you to set the value for this child page. The controls are different for each parameter type. For a string parameter (as you saw in the preceding section), there's just a single text field. For a color parameter, there is also a color picker, and for a boolean parameter, there is a checkbox, and so on.

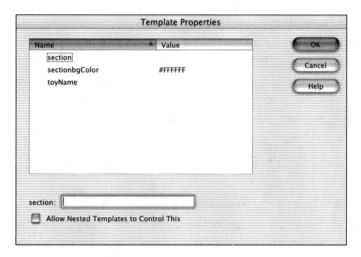

Figure 3.15   The Template Properties dialog.

Note that this dialog will not call any real bounds checking on your parameters. For example, if you enter a section name that is not in your store, this dialog will not report an error—it will just accept the string value.

There is one more control in this dialog: the Allow Nested Templates to Control This checkbox (see Figure 3.16). If you enable this checkbox, the other controls for the parameter disappear, and the word (passthrough) appears in the list. What's this?

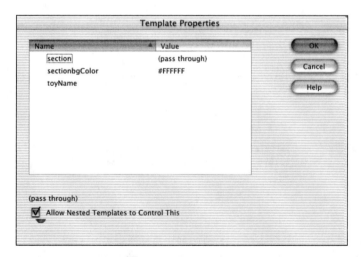

Figure 3.16   Template Properties with parameter set as passthrough.

Passthrough Parameters

A *passthrough parameter* is a parameter that doesn't affect anything in its second generation of nested templates, but affects only things in their child pages (that is, third-generation pages with respect to the original template). Let's have an example: Suppose that you want to have a base template for your entire site, whose whole job was to impose some three-column formatting and perhaps a logo. You would then make nested templates as child templates of this base template for all of the different template pages in the site. In this case, the toy product page would itself be a nested template of this base layout template.

Suppose, when you set up the base template, you decide that all pages on the site will have a 'section' parameter. It would make sense to define it in the base template, rather than having to remember to define it in each of the child templates. But there's a problem here. When you create the child templates, they are going to want to set the value of this parameter, and then they won't pass it through to their child pages (the pages the user actually sees). This is the way the DMX template engine works, remember? You run the program, output some HTML, and then the program (the template tags like the TemplateParam tag) is no longer visible in the child page. So there's no way to let the final child pages (the product pages themselves) control the section parameter, unless the parameter somehow "passes through" the child template. That's what this flag is for—it "shields" the parameters from the template program on the first instance of its use.

Let's run through that example again. Here's a new template, the base template, that includes the Hot Cool Toys logo, and three layout columns (see Figure 3.17).

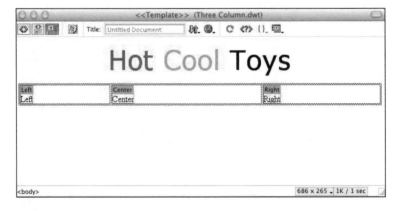

Figure 3.17   The Base Template.

It's not visible, but this template contains a `'section'` parameter, just as in the preceding example.

Next, make a child page of this template, and save it as a (nested) template. This will be the product page. In this page are three editable regions. Put the expression `"@@(section)@@"` into the left editable region.

Note that this editable region (left) is now no longer editable, as discussed later in this section. Using the Template Properties dialog, mark the `'section'` parameter as passthrough, and DMX will change the `InstanceParam` tag to look like what appears in Figure 3.18.

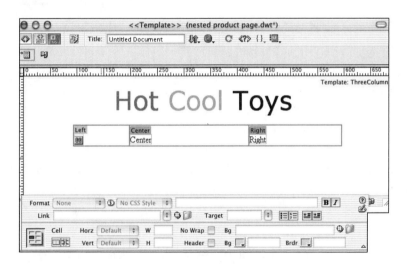

Figure 3.18   Left editable region locked (orange) and marked as passthrough (with @@ icon).

```
<!-- InstanceParam name="section" type="text" value="" passthrough="true" -->
```

Now, in an instance of this page, you can set the `"section"` parameter to something like `"preschool"`, and the child page looks like what appears in Figure 3.19.

Note that because there were no changes to the editable regions in the child template, they're still editable in this page. That's probably not what you would really want—they would probably be filled in with more template regions for the product page so that the page author has only to enter information about the specific product.

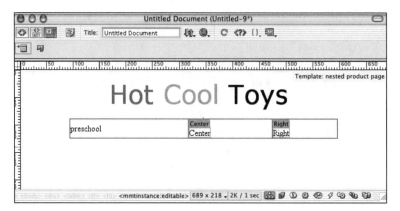

Figure 3.19   Document showing @@ symbol replaced by the Parameter value as defined using Modify > Template Properties.

One final thing about nested templates. Just as one might want to pass a parameter through a child template into the child pages, it is also possible to pass an expression itself from the parent to the children. For example, suppose the `section` parameter is made part of the headline for all pages in the Hot Cool Toys site. There needs to be a way to tell DMX not to run the expression when it's creating the child template (because the child template doesn't know what section it's in—the parameter hasn't been set yet). But, with existing methods, it would be necessary to enter the expression over and over in all the child templates (also, the headline is locked, and to do this it would have to be made editable).

In this case, there's another syntax for expressions, called the *passthrough expression syntax*. Instead of typing this:

`@@(section)@@`

use this:

`@@@(section)@@@`

The triple ampersand tells DMX to pass the expression through the first level of templates into the grandchild pages. That is, the expression isn't evaluated in the child template; rather, it's converted from a triple ampersand, into a double and evaluated in the child page of the child template.

> **Note**
>
> These preceding paragraphs are a dense bit of explanation here. We admit that each careful read-through invariably leads to head-scratching. To help with this, we are providing a hierarchy of testing templates called `layout.dwt`, `layout2.dwt`, and `layout3.dwt` in the book site. These are simple pages offering three generations of nested templates, with a few optional and editable regions. You can use these files to investigate the way passthrough parameters work, and we encourage you to do so.

An optional region can contain any valid HTML or dynamic code. For instance, it can contain a table row, an image, a Flash file, a datum extracted from a database, or just about anything else. It cannot, however, contain a single table cell.

To add an optional region to your template, select Insert > Template Objects > Optional Region. The New Optional Region dialog opens, as shown in Figure 3.20. You also can right-click in the document's Code or Design view, bring up the context menu, and select Template > New Optional Region.

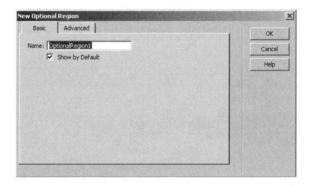

Figure 3.20   New Optional Region dialog—Basic tab.

In this dialog panel, you see basic and advanced tabs. Using the options on these tabs allows some direct control of the optional regions in child pages.

The Basic tab prompts for your input of a name for the region in DMX's Design view and in the region's associated controlling template parameter in the head (although this is not clear from the wording on the dialog). Observe your operating system's naming conventions here and use no special characters.

The Show by Default checkbox (pertinent only to a Boolean type region) allows you to specify the default state of the optional region; that is, true or false. When this is checked, the region will be shown in the child pages; when unchecked, it will not be shown.

Note

Inserting an optional region in this way will *only* insert this region with `type="boolean"`. To insert any other type of optional region (text, number, color, URL) will require either using one of the snippets provided by installing the Snippet Extension or manually editing the template markup inserted by DMX, because DMX's UI provides no access to these other types.

The Advanced tab allows you to control the display of the optional region using two methods:

- You can link it to a parameter already defined on the page by choosing the Use Parameter radio button. The associated drop-down is populated with a list of parameters already defined on the page and allows this new region's display to be controlled by a parameter that has already been defined by selection of the desired parameter from the list.

- It can be linked to the value of a template expression. By selecting the Use Expression radio button, you can define this expression in the associated text area (see the template expressions discussion for more information).

The display of the optional region in any child page will be dependent on the result of either method 1 or 2 (see Figure 3.21).

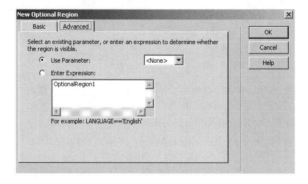

Figure 3.21   New Optional Region—Advanced tab.

There are several things to note about this dialog:

- The Basic and Advanced tabs are mutually exclusive. In other words, you can use one or the other, but not both for any given optional region. The tab displayed when the panel is opened is dependent on which tab had visibility when the OK button was last clicked.

- When the OK button is clicked with the Basic tab visible, a Boolean template parameter is added to the head of the document.

- When the OK button is depressed with the Advanced tab visible, no new template parameter is created. By using the Advanced tab, you link the region's display to either the value of an existing template parameter (selected from the list) or the result of a template expression (entered manually).

- Whether you define an optional region using the Basic tab or the Advanced tab, the code that is added to the template is nominally the same: Other than the differences mentioned earlier, the only thing that is different is whether an expression is added to the optional region markup.

Basic markup:

```
<!-- TemplateParam name="OptionalRegion1" type="boolean" value="true" -->
(added to the HEAD)
<!-- TemplateBeginIf cond="OptionalRegion1" -->OptionalRegion1
<!-- TemplateEndIf --> (added to the BODY)
```

Advanced Markup—Use Parameter:

```
<!-- TemplateBeginIf cond="DWT_Test" -->DWT_Test<!-- TemplateEndIf -->
(added to the BODY)
```

Advanced Markup—Expression:

```
<!-- TemplateBeginIf cond="language=='English'" -->Content
<!-- TemplateEndIf --> (added to the BODY)
```

By selecting the optional region markup (in either Code or Design view), the Property inspector is populated with an Edit button which, once clicked, displays the New Optional Region dialog so that you can edit the optional region. This also works if you select the <mmtemplate:if> in the Tag Selector.

Using Expressions in Optional Regions

In addition to controlling the display of an optional region using parameters, you can also use an expression, for example:

```
<!-- TemplateBeginIf cond="(section=='preschool') && (toyName=='Elmo' ||
toyName=='Bert')" -->
Hey!
Just for Preschool! It's @@(toyName)@@
<!-- TemplateEndIf -->
```

In this case, the optional region would be displayed if and only if the section name is preschool and the toyName is Elmo or Bert.

Using Expressions to Make "Implicit" Optional Regions

Often, you will have content that should appear in several places in a page. For example, you might want to have the section name appear at the top of the page but also appear in a navigation link at the bottom of the page. In these cases, it is very convenient to reference the expression itself. You can use either the tag syntax or the @@ syntax for this. First, let's add some HTML to the top of a page:

```
You are browsing in @@(_document.section)@@
```

Next, let's create breadcrumbs at the bottom of a page to let the user navigate.

```
<p><a href="home.html">Home</a> &gt; <a href="@@(section +
'.html')@@">@@(section)@@</a></p>
```

What does all this do? First, we inserted a link to the home page. Then we inserted a link that will be written when the page is generated. Note that there are two expressions in this link. The first one uses the value of the 'section' parameter to generate the target of the link (which, in our preschool example would be 'preschool.htm'). The second expression simply outputs the value of the 'section' parameter itself. The final result after the expression is processed by the template program looks something like this in the child page:

```
<a href="Home.htm">Home</a> C¦ <a href="preschool.htm">preschool</a>
```

By specifying "stacked" optional regions, you can create a series of tests that would permit a modest decision tree. For example,

- If condition 1, then display element 1
- If condition 2, then display element 2
- If condition 3, then display element 3

Not only are constructions like this tedious to read and decipher, they also are slower to evaluate during child page creation, because each condition must be evaluated, even if the first is true. Moreover, should any "normal" code inadvertently be inserted between the condition statements of such constructions, things are likely to become unpredictable. But, there is a better way. Read on!

MultipleIf Optional Regions

Wow! Optional regions on steroids and also part of the conditional region group! MultipleIf optional regions avoid all of the problems mentioned earlier. Unfortunately, there is no user interface for adding them; instead, you must add them to your template by hand. Using the `TemplateSnippets` extension, you will have access to the MultipleIf optional region as well in the Templates > If group (`M_Block`)—and it will be *simple*!

Note

Please note that the Macromedia-supplied help file, which you can access by pressing F1, contains errors in the code area of the documentation, although the associated instructions are OK. Macromedia has since made corrections to this text and these corrections are available at the following area of the Macromedia web site: `www.macromedia.com/support/dreamweaver/documentation/using_dwmx_help_err ata/index.html`. Please note that their errata is still incorrect in some places and will be corrected soon—probably by the time you read this manuscript.

The main difference between the optional region already described and the MultipleIf region is that the MultipleIf region is parsed by the template engine only until it finds a condition which evaluates as true. At this point, the remainder of the conditional clauses are abandoned, which can mean a slight performance gain in creating your template based site. A final difference is that a MultipleIf optional region is far easier to find on the page for troubleshooting than are a group of optional regions, just because of the visual appearance.

Just as with optional regions, MultipleIf regions reference a template parameter defined in the head of the document. This reference can be to a parameter that has already been defined, or it can be to one you have created specifically for use by this region.

```
<!-- TemplateBeginMultipleIf -->
 <!-- TemplateBeginIfClause cond="" --> Insert Output 1
 <!-- TemplateEndIfClause -->
 <!-- TemplateBeginIfClause cond="" --> Insert Output 2
 <!-- TemplateEndIfClause -->
 <!-- TemplateBeginIfClause cond="" --> Insert Output 3
 <!-- TemplateEndIfClause -->
 <!-- TemplateBeginIfClause cond="" --> Insert Output 4
 <!-- TemplateEndIfClause -->
<!-- TemplateEndMultipleIf -->
```

Above, you see a blank MultipleIf region added by the snippet. This particular code block has four conditional statements, or `if` clauses. Each clause must be unique and can contain a simple or a complex expression, both for the conditional test and for the output. For instance, in the following example, we have a parameter named `"digit"` with `type="number"` and a default (initial) value of `0`.

```
<!-- TemplateParam name="digit" type="number" value="0" -->
<!-- TemplateBeginMultipleIf -->
 <!-- TemplateBeginIfClause cond="digit==1" --> 1 "
 <!-- TemplateEndIfClause -->
```

```
<!-- TemplateBeginIfClause cond="digit==2" --> 2
<!-- TemplateEndIfClause -->
<!-- TemplateBeginIfClause cond="digit==3" --> 3
<!-- TemplateEndIfClause -->
<!-- TemplateBeginIfClause cond="digit==4" --> 4
<!-- TemplateEndIfClause -->
<!-- TemplateEndMultipleIf -->
```

Note

Be aware that the requirement to enclose parameter values in quotation marks over-rides the intuitive sense that a value should not be quoted:

```
<!-- TemplateParam name="digit" type="number" value="0" -->
```

Instead of this:

```
<!-- TemplateParam name="digit" type="number" value=0 -->
```

To effect this series of tests, you create the child page and adjust the value of "digit" using Modify > Template Properties:

A detailed description of the logic would work something like this:

- If the value is left at 0, nothing is displayed and no error is produced.
- If the value is changed to 1 through 4, the displayed item is the value of 1 through 4, respectively.
- If the value is changed to something not between 1 and 4 inclusively, the result is 0.

Is there a way to make sure that the child page user sets a valid value for the template parameter? Yes there is! Add another if clause to check for valid values. If no valid value is found, then display a warning message that you generate like this:

```
<!-- TemplateBeginIfClause cond="((digit<'1')||(digit>'4'))" --> Please
use a valid number between 1 and 4 <!-- TemplateEndIfClause -->
```

Because the initial value is 0, the warning message displays initially when the child page is created from the template. This is an excellent way to let the content editor know what the acceptable values are for that template region.

You can have other region types within each if clause! This can get very complex very fast, so experiment with this to see what works best for you. During testing, we had a MultipleIf region where the first option contained plain text, the next contained an editable region, the third contained a repeating region, and the last contained a repeating table—and it all worked wonderfully. To see this in action, take a look at the template named `multipleIfTest.dwt` in the `SectionI.zip` archive that you downloaded.

Editable Optional Regions

Similar to optional regions, editable optional regions are part of what could be thought of as the conditional region group. An editable optional region added to the template page is fully visible only on the template pages. They are visible on a child page depending on the value of its associated parameter and when set to `'show'`, only the contents of the optional region and the editable region contained within will be displayed.

You can insert editable optional regions in block mode only using Design or Code view. If there is something currently selected, this region type is inserted immediately after the current selection.

A work-around here is to select your content, and insert an optional region. If the content becomes deselected, select it again, this time inserting an editable region. Your content is now positioned inside an editable optional region, although it took you a few more mouse clicks to get there. This same work-around applies if you want to have UI control of the inserted editable region name because when this menu item is selected, the presented UI only prompts you for the optional region name and not the contained editable region name. You can, of course, manually change the contained editable region name in Code view or use the Tag Selector and Property Inspector.

How Do You Recognize Editable Optional Regions?

Editable optional regions insert two segments of code into the template; one in the `<head>` area and one in the `<body>` area. The `<head>` content is a template parameter. The `<body>` content is identified by the following code (it's actually inserted on the page as one line of code):

```
<!-- TemplateBeginIf cond="OptionalRegionName" -->
  <!-- TemplateBeginEditable name="EditRegion3" -->
  ...
  <!-- TemplateEndEditable -->
<!-- TemplateEndIf -->
```

If the parameter in the `<head>` area of a child page has been set to `show`, you can identify editable optional regions in Code view by finding something similar to the following code:

```
<!-- TemplateBeginEditable name="EditRegion3" -->
...
<!-- TemplateEndEditable -->
```

In Design view, an editable optional region is identified in a manner similar to an editable region, with an outlining border containing a tab and the name of the region.

In a template, when an editable optional region is selected (or clicked), the Tag Selector displays `<mmtemplate:if><mmtemplate:editable>` or `<mmtemplate:if>` if your cursor is outside the editable region but still inside the optional region.

In a child page, the Tag Selector shows the result it displays for any normal editable region when the region is selected or clicked: `<mmtinstance:editable>`.

How Do You Work with Editable Optional Regions?

In a template page, you add a repeat region by selecting or clicking in an appropriate page element (refer to Table 3.3) and doing one of the following:

- Selecting Insert > Template Objects > Editable Optional Region
- Clicking the Editable Optional Region icon in the Insert Panel's Templates Tab

To delete an editable optional region, select the entire region by:

- Clicking the region name tab in Design view
- Selecting the `<mmtemplate:if>` tag on the Tag Selector
- Manually selecting the entire region's code in Code view, and then pressing the Delete key

Clicking within an editable optional region reveals both `<mmtemplate:if>` and `<mmtemplate:editable>` tags on the Tag Selector. Selecting the `<mmtemplate:if>` tag or the editable optional region's border tab selects the region, its contents, and its identifying comment tags. This means that selecting the tab and pressing the Delete key can delete an editable optional region, removing the region and its contents. On the other hand, you can delete an editable optional region by selecting the region and applying Modify > Templates > Remove Template Markup, which removes the "optional" part of the region, but not the region's contents which would include an editable region! Remove Template Markup is explored extensively in Chapter 4.

In a child page, you can neither add nor delete editable optional regions, but you can modify them by electing to show or not show them on the current page by using the all-too-familiar Modify > Template Properties menu item.

You can edit the contained editable region name exactly the same way you would edit a normal editable region, as outlined earlier in this chapter. You also can invoke the same for the parent optional region in exactly the same manner as the optional region discussed earlier.

You can use an editable optional region in such a manner that when you show it, the region can contain locked content and an editable area such as this:

```
<!-- TemplateBeginIf cond="OptionalRegionName" -->
  <p>This content would be locked (non-editable) on the child page!</p>
  <!-- TemplateBeginEditable name="EditRegion3" -->
  <p>This content would be editable on the child page</p>
  <!-- TemplateEndEditable -->
  <p>This content would also be locked(non-editable) on the child
  page!</p>
<!-- TemplateEndIf -->
```

That's all there is to it for editable optional regions. Their real utility comes mostly into play on a clean new document, but, as we have shown, you can manually add this region type anywhere in your template with ease. It just takes a few mouse clicks to do it!

Editable Tag Attributes

Any HTML <body> tag, including the body tag itself, can have one or more editable attributes assigned to it using DMX's new capabilities. Such editable attributes can include any legal attribute for the given HTML tag, or even illegal (proprietary) attributes. As a result, it is important to use this feature with caution and understanding.

An editable tag attribute is one that is defined in the template (using Modify > Templates > Make Attribute Editable) with the intention that each spawned child page can specify a unique value for that attribute. You make this specification using the Modify > Template Properties dialog on each child page. For example, you can make the source attribute of an <img> tag editable in a template, allowing each child page to display a different image in that location.

In addition to the usual tag attributes, an editable tag attribute also can be an event handler, like onload or onresize, and so on. Although it is beyond the scope of this book to provide a comprehensive discussion of tags and their attributes and event handlers, perhaps a simple example will illustrate the complexity and flexibility this option offers.

Consider the <body> tag, which in addition to the usual background, margin, and color attributes, often contains event handlers to trigger certain events, such as the DMX preloadImages behavior and the associated onload event handler. By making this onload "attribute" editable, you make it possible to specify the parameters that would be passed by that event handler to the associated JavaScript function on each child page.

Although this is possible, each set of parameters must be entered manually on each child page and is subject to entry errors, as might be expected.

To make a tag's attribute editable, use Modify > Templates > Make Attribute Editable after selecting the appropriate tag either in Code or Design view, using the methods already discussed (see Figure 3.22).

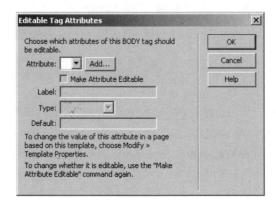

Figure 3.22   The Editable Tag Attribute dialog.

You will be using the following fields:

- **Attribute**—The Attribute field populates only with the attributes already specified within the selected tag on this template page, either static (hard-coded) or already defined as editable. If the list does not populate with an attribute that you want to use, click the Add button to add it to the list manually.

- **Add**—Use this button to add an attribute that you know works for the selected tag and is not defined in the drop-down to the left. A new dialog opens, prompting you for the attribute name. This is where you could add a proprietary attribute name. Figure 3.23 shows an attribute being added for the <body> tag (as mentioned previously).

After you click the OK button, the Attribute field populates with this added attribute (see Figure 3.24).

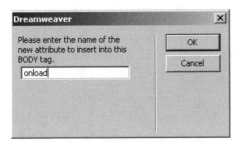

Figure 3.23   The Add Attribute dialog.

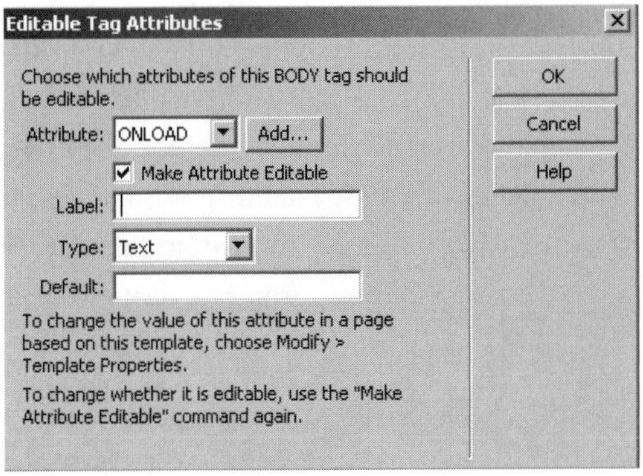

Figure 3.24   The Editable Tag Attribute dialog.

Be warned—there is no error-checking or validation performed while in this dialog! If you get JavaScript errors in your child page, this may be a good place to start looking. For instance, you could add a fictitious attribute of `mytagattrib` and the remainder of the dialog will function without error.

- **Make Attribute Editable**—Enabled by default, you can deselect this option if you want to hard-code the parameter value to force its use on the child page. It must be mentioned that we could find no practical value for disabling the Make Attribute Editable checkbox.

- **Label**—Using this field, you define the parameter name that you would like to assign for this editable tag. Use good naming practices because the value you type here will be used on the child page when you select Modify > Template Properties. The Modify Template Properties dialog is opened and populated.

- **Type**—This field allows you to specify the parameter type, which assists in determining valid input data using the Modify > Template Properties dialog.

Available choices are Text; URL; Color; True/False; and Number. Each of these types is discussed elsewhere in this chapter. If you have installed the TemplateSnippets extension, these options are available from the Templates > Parameters group in the snippets panel.

- **Default**—This field is optional. It can be left blank or you can enter your preferred default value for this parameter. As per our example, using the <body> tag and the onLoad attribute, we might want a default preload statement. So, in this field you would want to add the following line:

MM_preloadImages()

This will add the null preload function call to the onLoad event handler. The problem with this is that the actual preload JavaScript itself hasn't yet been added to the page. So you want to undo the add editable attribute, and then add the preload images behavior to the <body> tag using the Behavior panel. Then you want to select the <body> tag and make the onLoad attribute editable, which in turn would populate the default field with the required function call and also add the appropriate script to the page <head> region.

Warning

We can't stress enough that if you choose to add a null JavaScript function call manually on any tag event attribute, you *must* make sure that you add the relevant JavaScript block to the <head> area of the document, or JavaScript errors will occur!

Using an Expression Inside a Tag Attribute

You also can use an expression inside a tag attribute. For example, different sections of your site might have different color themes. For example, they might all have a different background color, link color, and so on. In the template file, you can control this by defining a new template parameter, perhaps background, and using this parameter in an expression in the body's bgColor attribute.

Select the <body> tag with the Tag Selector (or the Tag inspector), and use Modify > Templates > Make Attribute Editable to bring up the Editable Attributes dialog. An *editable attribute* is a tag attribute whose value in the child pages comes from the evaluation of a template expression. The attribute is said to be "editable" because, although the rest of the tag is locked in the child page, the author can change the value of the attribute by changing the values of the parameters used by the expression for that attribute.

In the Editable Attributes dialog, click Add to add an editable attribute. Enter bgColor, the attribute for background color for the <body> tag. The fields of the dialog look like Figure 3.25.

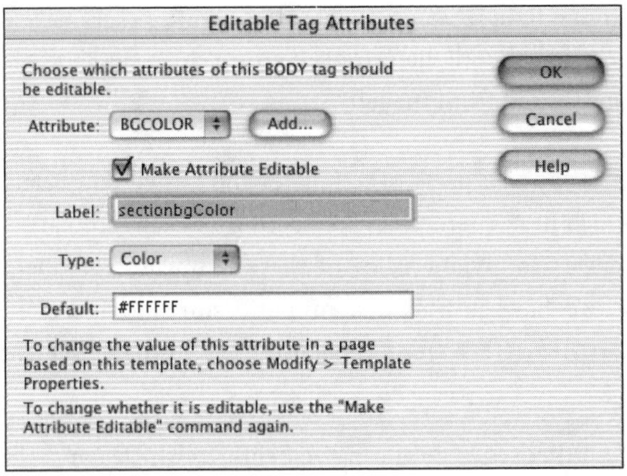

Figure 3.25   Completed Editable Tag Attribute dialog.

Fill in the label, type, and default values as shown in the figure. When you click OK, DMX will do two things. First, it will create a new template parameter called sectionBGColor. Second, it will write out this code into the BODY tag:

```
<body bgcolor="@@(sectionbgColor)@@">
```

You can add editable tag attributes to any tag and it can contain any values (there is not a controlling user interface, per se), so you must know your HTML to use this template function effectively without causing errors on your child pages. Remember that there is no validation performed to ensure that you are using an allowable attribute for the tag or that the default value is usable.

Nesting Templates

Nested templates are completely new in DMX. They happen when you create a template, spawn a child from that template, and save the child as a template. Using nested templates allows you, as the developer, to control editable regions and their content in child templates. In order to understand the utility of nested templates and see how they might improve your efficiency as a developer, it is important to be clear about how regions, parameters, and expressions behave in nested templates and their child pages.

Creating Nested Templates

There are two ways to create a nested template:

- Create your initial template and save it. Then create a child page of this template and select File > Save As Template. This saved document becomes your nested template.

- Create your initial template and save it. Then create a child page of that template, open the Insert bar, choose the Template group, and select the Make Nested Template icon (second from the left).

If your site contains a complex array of templates and nested templates, you may find it difficult to track which nested templates are based on which templates. Using a naming convention that reflects the relationship of these templates may help in these cases. Keeping it simple, we have just used a numeric suffix to indicate the generation. For example, `layout3.html` is a third-generation HTML page, the child of a second-generation template.

There seems to be no theoretical limit on the depth to which templates can be nested; however, the practical limit is simply one of utility—how many levels of control do you need? Let's investigate what this means.

In the following discussion, we will refer to templates and their child pages using a generational reference; for example, the parent template is referred to as "generation 1." Its child pages are referred to as "generation 2," whether they are ordinary pages or nested templates. Child pages of second-generation pages will be called third-generation pages, and so on. This will help keep things straight for us all.

Using Nested Templates

In the absence of other controls, a second-generation nested template inherits all editable regions from its parent. Without further modification, this would not be a very useful thing, because the two template generations would produce the same child pages. The trick is to manage the editable regions so that they don't all pass to the child pages or so that their content either skips generations or stops propagating to generations. All of these are possible.

To really think about this, we have to train ourselves to think about the *child* pages, because it is those pages from which we actually build our sites. So each example we give will be illustrated in terms of how the method affects the child pages, either second or higher generations. Let's start with an easy example.

Suppose that you have a page with a variety of section-specific graphic elements, a navigation system, and a variable content region (see Figure 3.26). You want to use this page to build the entire site, but there is one section of the site that will have five or six separate pages within it. You want all these section pages to look the same, but you don't want to have to worry about making all the changes that might be necessary to spawn that specific version of the template page over and over again. In addition, you would have to build the master template in such a way that the specific graphic elements are open to editing at the child level. These two requirements are possible but perhaps tediously difficult in DW. DMX offers an opportunity to make this much easier.

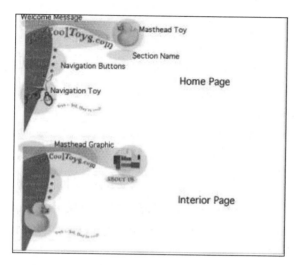

Figure 3.26   Simple layout plan showing editable content area.

Without nested templates, you would have to make multiple child pages of the master template, adjust each of these child pages to the specific graphic configuration of the section being built, and then add in the page-specific content.

With nested templates, you can spawn a child, adjust parameters in that child and get the graphic configuration set, save this child as a section template (that is, nested), and use it to spawn third-generation child pages for the particular section. That's much easier! The final page's configuration is set only once, and it is not as vulnerable to error as a result. In addition to this, the propagation of changes from parent to child across both generational templates will work exactly as expected.

See what we mean? This is a clear example of how nested templates can help.

If this is not totally clear yet, please re-read this section or continue on to Section II. Chapter 8 "Modifications to the Template," walks you through a complete example showing a couple of possible uses of nested templates.

Nested Regions

Let's add complexity to the topic by limiting what is editable in child pages. Suppose that you are on a page in the example just given and you realize that you need to add some section-specific information that will change periodically. You could simply add this information at the top of the content editable region, but not only is it vulnerable to inadvertent modification in a child page, it also is not subject to "propagation control" by a template as long as it is in an editable region. In other words, because this section-specific information is in an editable region, to change it you need to either make changes on each page in that section or use a find-and-replace operation in the third-generation child pages. But DMX offers an alternate method.

In the second-generation template page, insert the specific content in the content editable region. Now, insert another editable region beneath this content, yet within the first-editable region. When you do this in a second-(or higher) generation template (that is, insert an editable region in an editable region), the parent editable region becomes un-editable in its child pages and subject to template control! This is cool. By nesting editable regions (in a second-or-higher generation template), it is possible to control what is exposed to developer modification at that generation's child level. Nested editable regions can be added at any generational level to achieve this control.

> **Note**
> You cannot nest regions like this in a first-generation template page. Attempting to do so will produce a nag from DMX reminding you that The selection is already in an editable, repeating or optional region.

Remember that we said that we were going to look at how to make template content skip generations? In a sense, we have done that, in that a nested editable region causes the content in the outer region to be un-editable in the second-generation child pages. But to really do that (that is, without nesting editable regions), we have to look at how parameters behave in nested templates.

Parameter Passthrough

Create a new page as a basic HTML template. Drag a layer on this page and name the layer parameterLayer. Position it somewhere near the middle of the page and give it a distinctive background color. Select parameterLayer and then wrap it in an optional region by using Insert > Template Objects > Optional Region. Name the optional region **"testLayer"** using the Basic tab, and leave the Show by Default checkbox enabled. Click OK. To avoid being continually prompted about templates not having editable regions, insert another layer somewhere on the page, and make its contents editable. You can use your imagination to name both this layer and its contained editable region. Save this template using File > Save As Template. (I used layout.dwt as the filename.)

Use this template (layout.dwt) to spawn two child pages. Save one child page as a (nested) template again with File > Save As Template (I used layout2.dwt as the filename), and the other as an ordinary child page (I used layout2.html). Note that the 2 in the filename indicates that both pages are second-generation pages. Spawn a third-generation child from layout2.dwt, and save it (I used layout3.html).

Now you are ready for some interesting stuff. Open layout3.html and note that parameterLayer is visible, but if you try to change that by using Modify > Template Properties, you are told No template properties available. Remember that when you insert an optional region, you also cause a parameter with that region's name to be inserted in the head of the document. This happens because the parameter called "testLayer" is fixed in value by the DMX template program when it spawns the third-generation child page.

Look at the code for layout3.html and you will see that there is no parameter definition in the head of the document (again, this is removed by the template program when spawning the third-generation page). You can track this parameter by looking at the code on the pages—it is present in layout2.html, but not in layout3.html. So, it is possible to control the display of this layer in second-generation child pages (using Modify > Template Properties), but not in third-generation child pages. This is useful in cases where you want some page element to appear or not appear on all second-generation pages, but once its visibility is set, you do not want it to be further adjusted in subsequent generations.

Note
You cannot use Modify > Template Properties in a first-generation template page. Attempting to do so will reveal that the option is simply not available from the Modify menu.

Suppose that you need to control this optional region's visibility in the third-generation pages but not in the second-generation pages. That is where the passthrough parameter comes into play. Try this: Open layout2.dwt, use Modify > Template Properties, and select "testLayer" as the parameter to adjust (depending on what you have done in your experimentation, you may have other parameters on this page). When you select this parameter, you should see the Allow Nested Templates to Control This checkbox appear toward the bottom of the page. By selecting this checkbox, you are invoking the passthrough parameter. Go ahead and select the checkbox, and click OK. You should see a new region added to the page that wraps the parameterLayer's anchor icon called

"PassthroughIf", and if you look at the Code view for the page, you should see something like this in the body:

```
<!-- TemplateBeginPassthroughIf cond="testlayer" -->
<div id="parameterLayer" style="position:absolute; left:116px; top:73px;
width:86px; height:51px; z-index:1; background-color: #9900CC; layer-
background-color: #9900CC; border: 1px none #000000;"></div>
<!-- TemplateEndPassthroughIf -->
```

and this in the head:

```
<!-- InstanceParam name="testlayer" type="boolean" value="true"
passthrough="true" -->
```

When you set the passthrough parameter like this, you are disabling modifications of that parameter in the current generation and enabling modifications in the succeeding generation—but *only* in the succeeding generation. This quality of passthrough is detailed in Tables 3.4, 3.5, and 3.6.

Table 3.4   Without Passthrough

Filename/Type	Parameter Exposure
Generation1/template	Not Exposed
Generation2/template	Exposed
Generation2/file	Exposed
Generation3/template	Not Exposed
Generation3/file	Not Exposed
Generation4/template	Not Exposed
Generation4/file	Not Exposed

Table 3.5   With Passthrough Enabled Second Generation

Filename/Type	Parameter Exposure
Generation1/template	Not Exposed
Generation2/template	Not Exposed
Generation2/file	Exposed
Generation3/template	Exposed
Generation3/file	Exposed
Generation4/template	Not Exposed
Generation4/file	Not Exposed

Table 3.6   With Passthrough Enabled Second- and Third-Generation

Filename/Type	Parameter Exposure
Generation1/template	Not Exposed
Generation2/template	Not Exposed
Generation2/file	Exposed
Generation3/template	Not Exposed
Generation3/file	Exposed
Generation4/template	Exposed
Generation4/file	Exposed
Generation5/template	Not Exposed
Generation5/file	Not Exposed

Several things are quite clear from these tables. Enabling `passthrough` will delay exposure of the parameter until the next generation. Also, it is possible to stack `passthroughs` in successive generations. For example, by enabling `passthrough` in the second- and the third-generation templates, the parameter is not exposed until the fourth-generation template. Finally, the `passthrough` setting affects files differently than it does templates. Although DMX will allow you to select the Allow Nested Templates to Control This checkbox in a non-template child page, doing so has no effect on anything template-wise, and it probably should not even be there. But once the parameter has lost exposure, it is no longer available to either files or templates.

By using the Allow Nested Templates to Control This checkbox, you can continue to pass the parameter to each subsequent generation's child pages. When you reach a generation where this `passthrough` should stop, leaving the Allow checkbox unchecked will force evaluation of the parameter in child pages, and continued `passthrough` will stop with that generation. This facility allows you, the developer, to establish where that point will occur in the hierarchy of your nested templates.

Expression Evaluation and Passthrough

A template expression is evaluated at the time that the template program is run. The results of that evaluation are placed in the child page. In a sense, then, these template expressions are "transient" critters, lasting only long enough to be evaluated once, and then discarded.

But think about this for a moment. You have put the template expression on the page because you want it to do something. If this expression were put into an editable region, however, the expression itself would be subject to perhaps inadvertent editing, with potentially catastrophic results. Therefore, putting *any* template expression into an editable region in a template file will lock that region, which then becomes non-editable in all subsequent child generations, including child templates. But this is getting a little ahead. There are some restrictions on using expressions in templates, as discussed here:

- You *cannot* put a template expression into a first-generation template page's editable region. If you do this and then save the template document, DMX will warn you that ...`@@(...)@@ directives cannot be used inside editable regions.`

You *can* put a template expression into a first-generation template page's non-editable regions. It is evaluated and the results of that evaluation are propagated to all second-generation child pages, including second-generation templates. If the results of the evaluation are dependent on the value of a template parameter, by changing that parameter in these second-generation pages, you can affect the results of the evaluation, which will then appear on those second-generation pages (subject to the `passthrough` setting for that parameter, described previously). Beyond the second-generation, you will not be able to affect this evaluation at all, once again subject to the `passthrough` settings.

Obviously, you cannot put a template expression into a second- or higher generation non-editable region because those regions are simply not accessible in second- or higher generations.

You can (and perhaps should) put a template expression into a second (and higher) generation template's editable region. Depending on the expression, this may render the editable region partially or wholly non-editable. This is another way to affect editable regions and their accessibility in subsequent generations.

You can put a "null expression" —`@@(" ")@@`—into a second (or higher) generation template page. The effect of this will be to immediately render that editable region uneditable in third-generation page. The affected editable region will be still editable in the second-generation template page.

You can put a non-null expression that does not reference a template parameter into any editable region in any generation page.

You can put a non-null expression—`@@(...)@@`— into a second (or higher) generation template page, but only if you then use Modify > Template Properties and set any referenced template parameter to `passthrough`. If the expression references a template parameter and the parameter is *not* set to `passthrough`, the following error message is produced:

...`access to undefined template parameter "<parametername>"`

If the expression does not contain a reference to a template parameter, there are no restrictions.

Although the preceding restrictions have focused on using the @@ syntax for these expressions, the same restrictions would apply to the alternate comment-based template expression syntax.

Editing Code Outside of HTML Tags

There is a final "region" that should be mentioned in this chapter—code that falls outside the `<html></html>` tags; that is, Server Code. Previous versions of DW are not so kind to this code: If such code is changed in a template page with existing child pages, these changes are not propagated because the code is not in a non-editable region. Clearly this is not the correct way to deal with such server code, because it can cause unexpected and potentially disastrous errors.

To correct this, DMX enables the use of a new region outside the HTML part of a template page by recognizing the following comment:

```
<!-- TemplateInfo codeOutsideHTMLIsLocked="true | false" -->
```

This code shows that the value for the `codeOutsideHTMLIsLocked` variable can have either `'true'` or `'false'` as values.

To quote from the Help file in DMX,

> "When this code is present in a Template, changes to scripts before the `<html>` tag or after the `</html>` tag will be copied to documents based on that Template. However, you will no longer be allowed to edit those scripts in documents based on the Template. Thus, you can choose to be able to edit these scripts in the Template, or in documents based on the Template, but not both."

That's the good news. The bad news is that DMX has no UI devoted to altering this region. So, any changes here need to be done manually. We've provided an extension that consists of a snippet set for template-related code fragments. This particular snippet is in the Templates > Code Outside group in the Snippets panel: Select Enable to allow code above and below, and then select Disable to lock code above and below.

DMX's normal procedure is to create child pages with the `codeOutsideHTMLIsLocked` variable set to `"false"`. This means that the `'region'` above `<html>` or below `</html>` would be treated like any other editable region—that is, not propagated. In other words, you could freely add server code to any child page. If, however, you want this "outside" code to be propagated as though it were a non-editable region (meaning that you have a single bit of server code which is repeated in multiple child pages and you want to manage it from a single template page), you must manually edit the Template file to add this comment line anywhere in the <head> region:

```
<!-- TemplateInfo codeOutsideHTMLIsLocked="true" -->
```

Creating a child page from this Template will add the comment

```
<!-- InstanceBegin template="/Templates/outsidehtml_test.dwt.asp"
codeOutsideHTMLIsLocked="true" -->
```

which will instruct DMX to *not* allow changes to this region in child pages and to propagate changes to this region from the Template page.

Be very careful about how you use this template feature!

Updating a Template's Child Page

What happens if you made a modification to your template and then elect not to update the site? As with many other things, you can do it later!

There are two methods that you can use to update either a page or an entire site, and these will be discussed in the following sections.

The Modify Menu System

With a child page open, if you select Modify > Templates, you will be presented with two choices. The first is Update Current Page. When you select this option, the non-editable region(s) on this page are checked against the corresponding template's non-editable region(s), and the child is updated where required. The only indications that the job is done is that the document is given focus for editing, and the "dirty" flag is set (the asterisk following the filename indicates that the file has been changed and therefore needs to be saved).

The other option is Update Pages. When you select this menu item (with either child or template pages open), the Update Pages dialog opens (similar to that shown in Figure 3.27). Here you can choose to update the entire site or selected files containing a specific library item, or files that are children of a specific template file, as chosen in the Look in: fields. Operation of this dialog panel is similar to that already described for library items.

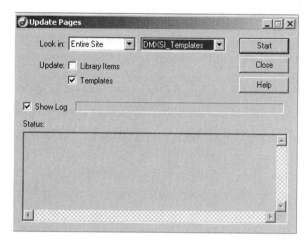

Figure 3.27   The Update Pages dialog.

The Template Assets Context Menu

This context menu functions completely analogously to that already described for library items in Chapter 2. Please refer to the discussion in that section for more descriptive information.

Using the Apply Template Function

There are four methods of accessing this function (all of which are disabled if no document is open and active):

- From the menu bar, select Modify > Templates > Apply Template to Page.
- Drag and drop the Template onto the open document from the Assets panel, Template category.
- Using the Templates category of the Assets panel, select the desired Template, right-click (Ctrl+click) to bring up the context menu and click Apply.
- Using the Assets Panel > Templates category, select the desired template, and click the Apply button in the lower-left corner of the panel.

The Apply Template menu is shown in Figure 3.28.

When to Use This Method

We highly recommended that you use the Apply Template function only to apply a template with a different layout to an existing template child page (these can be in the same site or in a different site) *only* if both templates have *exactly* the same editable region names. If there are any editable region names that differ, the page will not convert to the new template very well, leading to incorrect positioning or in the worst case, potential (inadvertent) data loss. You should never use this method to bring an external (non-template based) page into your site's template structure! There are quite a few quirks with it and there are more powerful and reliable methods to import data into a single template-based site. (Read the sections entitled "Export Template Data as XML" and "Import XML into Template" in Chapter 5 for more information.)

Figure 3.28
Apply Template Menu.

You could use this method to apply a template to a non-template based page if (this is a very strong **if**) you have text with only image links in the existing document. We strongly discourage you from applying a template to your page if your existing page contains any sort of navigation or structural layout.

Quirk 1: Both templates should have exactly the same editable region names or page data loss could occur (just because of the way one must specify where to put all content on the page). If there are any differences in region names, you must specify where the extraneous content gets placed using the Inconsistent Region Names Dialog (see Figures 3.29 and 3.30).

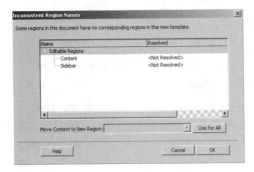

Figure 3.29   Inconsistent Region Names dialog.

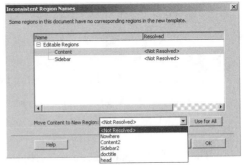

Figure 3.30   Inconsistent Region Names Dialog showing possible destination areas.

Quirk 2: When you are applying it to a non-template based page, this method imports the entire source document into the template's designated editable region, chosen using DMX's interface. Unfortunately, because the incoming document is not a templated document, it contains only two regions: `"Document body"` and `"Document head"`. How you manage these two regions will depend on what you elect to do in this process.

For Document head, select `Nowhere` or `head` as the target region. The former will discard that region's content. By selecting the latter, you are risking unnecessary duplication of head content at worst, and at best you will add some meta tags that may be appropriate such as description and keywords.

For Document body, select `Nowhere` (which would be a little strange), or the desired target region (because you are applying a template that could already contain one or more editable regions, you may have multiple choices here). By selecting `Nowhere`, as before, the content is discarded, thereby leaving you with an original copy of the template file (with the exception of new code that may have been added to the head region)! By selecting a target region, your *entire* original page is imported into the selected target region, perhaps producing a rather "stunning" page.

There is not a better method for trying various templates on a child page (to test different layouts for a future site update, for example); however, there is a much better method to bring external (non-template based) pages into a template that we will explore later in this chapter.

When Not to Use This Method

Avoid using the Apply Template function when bringing external pages into the template-based design, although it can be done (as explained earlier). With the much improved menu options of Export Markup (with XML), Export as XML and Import XML into Template, Apply Template is all but useless for importing non-template based pages!

Warnings

Be careful of the following events that might occur when using this method:

- Apply Template does not allow a finer "granularity" of insertion of page data into more than the two generic editable regions: `Document head` and `Document body`.

- Imports all the page's body content into the chosen target editable region. If that page has anything other than raw content, the import will produce less than desirable results, which will require a lot of clean-up time (that is, longer production time and higher costs for your client).

- Runs the risk of duplication of content, be it head content such as meta language, JavaScript, or even worse—having the entire page layout inside the editable region thereby duplicating the content of the non-editable regions of the template file (and producing a mess).

Summary

Well, thanks for sticking with us through this monster chapter. By now you should know about all of DMX's special template regions and how to manipulate them. Although there is still quite a bit more to go, you have gotten past the most challenging part and should now be ready for the fun coming soon.

We have covered the usual editable and non-editable regions. You have discovered that the template page can also contain repeat regions and repeat tables, which are simply content regions that may or may not be editable in child pages, but which can be repeated optionally on each page.

More importantly, though, we have gone deeply into the mind-bending intricacies of template parameters and how they can be used to control the display and formatting of content on the page. These parameters have limited interface in DMX, and in some cases, the only way to work with them is to take advantage of the snippets found on our support site. As a part of this study of template parameters, you have also learned to use template expressions, which will prove to be integral to your site layout for Hot Cool Toys. We encourage you to review these sections before launching into subsequent chapters if you are still feeling a little uncertain about your command of these options.

Finally, we closed out the chapter with a discussion of some miscellaneous aspects of template regions, such as code coloring, code highlighting, and several other menu options.

If you are ready to move on, let's do so!

Chapter 4

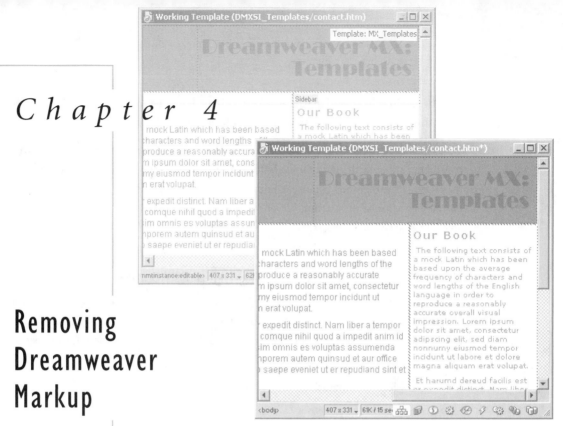

Before and After.

Removing Dreamweaver Markup

Dreamweaver Markup refers to those comments Dreamweaver inserts into templates, template child pages, and library items that allow Dreamweaver to control the various template regions discussed in Chapter 3, "All About Templates and Regions," and library items discussed in Chapter 2, "Library Items Revealed."

When you are building a template or using library items in Dreamweaver MX, HTML comments are embedded in the code for internal use by Dreamweaver, depending on the design-time methods you use. You may want to remove this markup before mounting the pages to the production server. In this chapter, we explore the techniques available and discuss their caveats.

Why Would You Want to Remove DMX Markup?

As discussed previously in Chapters 2 and 3, the DW/DMX template and library item markup is 100% proprietary, meaning that only DW/DMX can make appropriate use of it. You may want to remove DMX markup for various reasons, which include but are not limited to these:

- Bandwidth considerations
- Troubleshooting purposes
- Unique modifications
- Ability to conceal templates and libraries

The sections that follow explore these issues in more detail.

Bandwidth Considerations

Template and library markup can add a substantial amount of weight (bytes) to each document. By removing markup, you are reducing the page weight and therefore the bandwidth required for your site, which translates into faster load times for your individual pages and less expensive hosting costs if you're charged by bandwidth usage. This reduction is directly proportional to the number of template regions and library items on each page. A page with multiple repeat regions and multiple template parameters (particularly in a nested template) can become quite "bulky" due to the presence of this markup for each region and parameter.

Troubleshooting Purposes

Maybe you're having problems with a specific behavior that works in the template but not in the child page. Detaching the child page from the template would allow you to work 100% with the file without worrying about adding editable regions or editable tag attributes. Perhaps the troubleshooting is going to require help from an outside source such as a newsgroup member; in order for them to assist you efficiently, you should provide them with a copy of the child page and a detached child page so that they can work with the files in both forms to assist you. This admittedly is a very special case, and in most circumstances you would want to leave the markup intact to assist with locating the problem area more easily.

Unique Modification

On occasion, you might have a single page that you want to make unique, but still based on the original template. Detaching the page from the template will allow you to customize that unique page. This particular reason isn't so compelling anymore, given DMX's enhanced template capabilities.

Conceal the Use of Templates and Libraries

It's logical that you might build a site based on templates and library items for your own ease of maintenance. By detaching the child pages, you conceal the fact that you used a template to build the site.

Why Would You Want to Leave DMX Markup?

On the other hand, there are valid reasons to leave DMX's markup on the page. These include, but are not limited to, the following reasons:

- Remote co-workers
- Bandwidth
- Troubleshooting purposes

The following sections take a closer look at these considerations.

Remote Co-Workers

It's likely that you will eventually work collaboratively to build a site, if you aren't already. By leaving the markup intact on the page, it is easy for your remote or local co-worker(s) to make further modifications to the page without affecting the template or the updating functionality of DMX.

Bandwidth

The target market for the current site is the primary determinant with regard to Bandwidth concerns. Web developers are fortunate in that high-speed Internet services are becoming much more widespread and less expensive to use. Nevertheless, the population of dial-up users is not negligible in most demographics and is worthy of consideration. Depending on how extensively markup is used on the various pages of the site, you might be required to balance its removal against any productivity impact. Making markup removal the last operation prior to publishing the site may alleviate this concern.

Note

A modem making a connection at 56K has a theoretical maximum throughput of about 52,000 bits per second (due to telephone line restrictions). Some of this throughput is consumed with a "handshake" between the sending and receiving modems, although more of it is consumed by network congestion (lost and retransmitted packets). In practice, the typical 56K dialup connection can sustain a throughput of about 32,000 bits per second. With an 8-bit byte, this is equivalent to 4,000 bytes per second, or 4K/sec.

Most usability experts agree that a 10-second download time for a given page (or a page's engaging content) is the desired target to prevent a site's visitors from "clicking through," or leaving the site. This means that the target weight for any particular page should be 40–45K to meet this standard.

It is worth mentioning that corporate users are usually less concerned about bandwidth because most are on high-speed LANs and/or Internet connections. Therefore, in a corporate environment the internal documentation provided by the markup would be more beneficial than the bandwidth saved.

Troubleshooting Purposes

If you're having problems with a child page, leaving the markup intact could help you determine whether the issue is with a marked up region, thereby pointing you to the problem area (such as a specific library item or template region). Using the markup as a code commenting technique is ill-advised and not a replacement for good code commenting strategies, a discussion of which is beyond the scope of this book.

Methods of Removing Markup

As with many functions in DMX, there are different ways to remove markup. However, unlike other processes, each method of removing template markup is unique in what it actually does with the page and/or site.

Warning

Exercise caution using any of these methods. It is all too easy to inadvertently overwrite good pages with bad ones and to lose the template/library item update capability in a site. Unless you are careful with the options, an unintended export operation could overwrite finished pages! So choose your options carefully, and always perform a backup of your site prior to using these markup removal techniques.

Commands > Clean Up HTML

The first method of markup removal you need to learn is the Clean Up HTML command. To access this menu item (disabled if no document is open), select Commands > Clean Up HTML menu item to activate the Clean Up HTML dialog box (see Figure 4.1). Exercise 4.1 works through how to use this menu item and illustrates what it does on a templates child page.

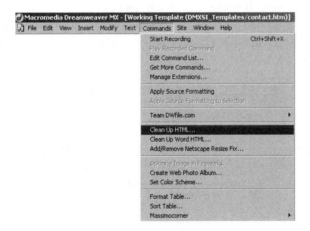

Figure 4.1   Clean Up HTML Menu.

You could use this method if you wanted a level of control to delete all template markup and do a code check at the same time, all while working on a single page that is based on a template. This method is usable only with the currently open and active document.

You cannot use this method if you desire your whole site to be affected. If you want to export your whole site removing markup, then please read the section entitled "Export without Markup," later in this chapter.

Be careful of the following events that might occur when using this method:

- This option works with an open and active document only.

- Depending on your Clean Up HTML dialog box settings, you could potentially disable functionality of the page.

- If you overwrite your template child page, it is difficult to get it back.

- The affected open and active document is not saved automatically, so no changes are written to the site until you save the file. (This is actually also a benefit because it allows you a level of error checking.)

Exercise 4.1:   Using Cleanup HTML to Remove Dreamweaver Markup

In this exercise, you'll see how to use the Clean Up HTML command by examining a practical example.

1. Make sure that you have the required site defined in DMX and that Dreamweaver is running—if not, then please see the instructions provided in the section entitled "Defining the Site" in the Section I, "Reusable Page Elements," or start Dreamweaver if your site is already defined.

2. Open the document named **contact.htm**, and then select the Commands > Clean Up HTML menu item. The Clean Up HTML dialog box should display (see Figure 4.2).

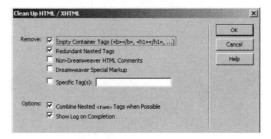

Figure 4.2   The Clean Up HTML Dialog box.

3. Place a checkmark in the checkbox beside Dreamweaver Special Markup. When you do this, a warning dialog box is displayed, as you can see in Figure 4.3.

Figure 4.3   Dreamweaver Special Markup Warning.

4. Click OK to close the warning box, and then click the OK button when you are satisfied with your selections. Dreamweaver will do its clean-up routine and clean the items you chose in step 3. When DMX is finished, it displays a

Summary Report telling you how many tags it removed from the active document (see Figure 4.4).

Figure 4.4   Clean Up Summary Report.

5. Save the changed file as **contact_clean_a.htm**, close the document, and leave DMX open for the next exercise. The document is now detached from templates and library items completely and will not be updated further by modifications to the templates or library items.

Modify > Templates > Detach from Template

To access this menu item (it is disabled if no document is open or if the open document is not attached to a template), select Modify > Templates > Detach From Template to activate the detachment routine (see Figure 4.5). Exercise 4.2 works through how to use this menu item and what it does on a template's child page.

Figure 4.5   Detach From Template Menu.

Similar to the Clean Up HTML command, this method also works for only the currently open and active document. There are no dialogs to complete, no warning prompts to read and acknowledge—it's instantaneous and unforgiving. Unlike the Clean Up HTML method, library items are left untouched by this command.

You cannot use this method if you desire your whole site to be affected. This method removes only template related markup—it will not remove library item markup.

Note the following warnings (as stated earlier) when using this method:

- This method works with only the active open document.
- You potentially could disable functionality of the page.
- If you overwrite your template child page, it is difficult to get it back, as you will see in Chapter 5, "Miscellaneous Template-Related Functions."
- The affected open and active document is not automatically saved, so no changes are written to the site until you save the file. (This actually is also a benefit because it allows you a level of error checking and control.)

Exercise 4.2:   Detaching a Child Page from Its Template

In this exercise, we will illustrate the methods we feel are the best to use for detaching pages from templates

1. It's assumed that you have the required site defined in DMX and that Dreamweaver is running; if not, then please see the instructions provided in the section entitled "Defining the Site" in the Section I, or start Dreamweaver if your site is already defined.
2. Open the document named contact.htm. Select the Modify > Templates > Detach From Template menu item. DMX goes through its detach routine and provides no notification that it is finished other than the document becomes active again—although you can see that it has been detached because the editable regions disappear.
3. Save the changed file as **contact_clean_b.htm**, close the document, and leave DMX open for the next exercise. The document is now detached from the template completely and will not be updated further by modifications to the template. However, library items remain attached to the document and will be affected by library item updates.

Modify > Templates > Export Without Markup...

There might be times when you would want to remove all template markup from an entire site. This section will explain how to do this.

To access this menu item (disabled if no document is open and active), select Modify > Templates > Export Without Markup to activate the Export Without Markup dialog box (see Figure 4.6). Exercise 4.3 works through how to use this menu item and what it does on a Templates child page.

Figure 4.6   Export without Markup Menu.

You could use this method if you wanted a level of control to delete all template markup on the entire site, or if you changed files only since last export and you don't want to affect your local site files. This method is used for exporting changed files (since last export) or all files (overwriting what was previously exported).

Do not use this method if you want to detach only a single page from the template. Do not use this method if you want library item information to be removed, because this method removes only template markup and not library markup.

Keep the following things in mind when using this method:

- This method is a site-wide method, so do not use it if you only want to detach a single page from the template or a select group of files.

- Markup other than that used by the template function of DMX is not removed by this method.

- If you previously exported your site and are happy with several files, using this method could overwrite those files if you are not extremely careful setting the Dialog options.

- A new Site Definition must be created to use DMX's built-in FTP Client to send the files to the server.

Exercise 4.3:   Exporting the Site without Dreamweaver Markup

Here's where we discover how to use this site-wide operation. In this exercise, we will put all that we have learned about Export Without Markup into practical use through a generalized example.

1. Begin with the site defined and Dreamweaver open.

2. Open the document named contact.htm. Select the Modify > Templates > Export Without Markup menu item. The Export Site Without Template Markup dialog box is displayed (see Figure 4.7).

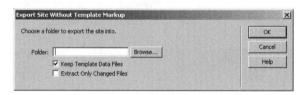

Figure 4.7   Export Without Markup dialog box.

In this dialog box, you'll see the following options:

- **Folder.** This entry must be a folder completely outside the current Dreamweaver Site Definition; otherwise, an error message will be displayed. The folder selection information is retained by the site once it is defined.

- **Keep Template Data Files.** This option creates XML template content files and saves them in the export folder in which the source file is located. These XML files can be used to import template data into a template-based page and can be used as a boilerplate for creating other template child pages, as you will learn in Chapter 6, "Building the Hot Cool Toys Base Template." This information is retained by the site.

- **Extract Only Changed Files.** This option extracts only those files that have changed since the last extraction. If an extraction has not occurred, this option extracts all child pages. This information also is retained by the site.

3. In the dialog box, fill in the fields as defined (see Figure 4.8):

   Folder: C:\DWT_Exported

   Keep Template Data Files: Enabled

   Extract Only Changed Files: Enabled

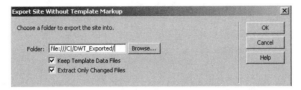

Figure 4.8   Export Without Markup dialog (Completed).

4. Depress the OK button, and Dreamweaver performs its magic magic by exporting the pages with all template markup removed.

Note

You would need to configure a second Site Definition to point to the exported site folder C:\DWT_Exported if you wanted to put these files to the server using Dreamweaver.

5. Close the document and leave DMX open for the next exercise. The site has now been detached from templates, possibly updated. The exported site will not be updated further by modifications to the templates or library items; however, the original site that you exported from will continue to be updated by changes to the template and/or library items.

Summary

In this chapter, you have learned various ways to detach a file or group of files from the template that created them. There are times when it's necessary or desirable to remove DMX's template and/or library markup. DMX offers you various solutions for your use, each method being unique in and of itself. Sometimes you decide that the best solution is to leave the markup on the pages. Should you desire a single page cleaned or a whole site, the choice is yours. ■

Chapter 5

Miscellaneous Template-Related Functions

Collage of commands.

Now that you're familiar with the major aspects of template, library item, and snippet functionality, it's time to learn about some of the finer points of these functions, including:

- Exporting as XML
- Importing XML into Templates
- Cloaking

Finishing off this chapter, you also learn some tips for using JavaScript that references URLs or images, Server Side Includes (SSIs), and Shockwave Flash (SWF) files with templates. Learning this will help you become more fluent and functional when making templates and using them to build small- to medium-sized web sites.

Export Template Data as XML

After completing the "Apply Template to Page" section of Chapter 4, "Removing Dreamweaver Comments," you can see the frustration that results from the amount of work it takes to get a page of content into your template-based structure. In this segment of the chapter, you learn the key advantage of using Export Template Data as XML with Import XML into Template to import multiple pages with minimal effort! The Export Template Data as XML option is shown in Figure 5.1.

The File > Export > Template Data as XML menu option allows you to export the template editable regions from the desired child page as an *.XML file. Later, you can edit this file multiple times and use it to add outside content into your template-based design (see the section, "The Exported XML File," later in this chapter).

After you are familiar with the format and structure of the XML file, you will be able to hand-code it with ease! Then, you will wonder why nobody ever pointed you in this direction when you asked, "How do I import a document into my template structure?"

The Template Data as XML option is disabled if no document is open or the currently active page is not derived from a template.

When to Use This Method

Use this method when you have one or more pages that are not linked to a template; you need them to be brought under a template's control, and you want to avoid the problems discussed above!

Figure 5.1
Export Template Data as XML menu.

> **Note**
>
> To use the File > Import > XML into Template option, you first need to either create the XML file by hand (YIKES!), use this command (ahhh!), or use Modify > Templates > Export Without Markup, with the Keep Template Data Files option enabled (covered in Chapter 3, "All About Templates and Regions").

When *Not* to Use This Method

You might not want to use this method in the following circumstances:

- You choose to use Apply Template as specified in Chapter 4.

- You choose to create a document with your content (No site layout; just standard P tags, for instance) and use Apply Template as specified in Chapter 4.

How to Use This Method

Exercise 5.1:   Export Template Data as XML

In this exercise, you put all that you have learned about Export Template as XML into practical use through a generalized example. This menu option is best used with the File > Import > XML into Template option.

1. It is assumed that you have the required site defined in DMX and that Dreamweaver is running. If necessary, please see the instructions provided in "Defining the Site" in Section I, or start Dreamweaver if your site is already defined.

2. Open the document named info.htm, and then select the File > Export > Template Data as XML option. The Export Template Data as XML dialog appears, as shown in Figure 5.2.

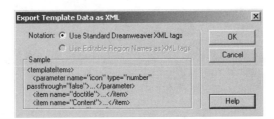

Figure 5.2   Export Template Data as XML dialog.

This dialog has two mutually exclusive options. The way to use these options is pretty easy once you get the hang of it.

If you have a child document containing one or more template parameters or repeating regions (as discussed in Chapter 4), use the Use Standard Dreamweaver XML tag option. (This radio button should be checked by default for this exercise; if it is not, please select this option.)

Note

During our testing, the Use Editable Region Names as XML tags option was disabled (grayed out) when the child page contained template parameters and/or repeating regions.

If you have a child document that does not contain template parameters or repeating regions, select the Use Editable Region Names as XML Tags option. In our testing, both options were enabled when the child page contained neither repeating regions nor template parameters.

3. Click the OK button and you will be prompted for the filename and path of the exported XML file (see Figure 5.3). Choose your local site folder—in this case, C:\DMXSI_Templates—and give the file a filename of info.xml. Click the Save button to save the file and close the dialog.

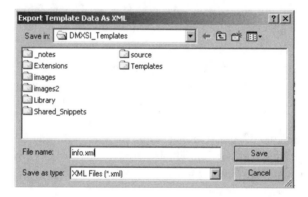

Figure 5.3   Export Template Data as XML dialog.

4. Close the document and leave DMX open for the next exercise. You have now successfully exported your template data as an XML file that you can use as a "template" for future content addition to the template-based design.

Warnings

Take care when you are editing the generated XML file. The File > Import > XML into Template option will not be at all happy with careless handling, and it will let you know by displaying error messages.

The Exported XML File

Now that you have generated an XML file that contains all your editable region information, we will go through the file line by line to show you, by example, what you can edit and what you should avoid.

info.xml Explored

Listing 5.1 shows the generated code from Exercise 5.1 (the file named info.xml). Areas that you can safely edit are highlighted in bold. All other areas should be avoided at all costs!

Listing 5.1   Generated Code from Exercise 5.1 (info.xml)

```
<?xml version="1.0"?>
<templateItems template="/Templates/MX_Templates.dwt"
codeOutsideHTMLIsLocked="false">
    <parameter name="icon" type="number"
passthrough="false"><![CDATA[2]]></parameter>
    <item name="doctitle"><![CDATA[
<title>Working Template</title>
]]></item>
    <item name="Content"><![CDATA[
        <h1>Information About Us</h1>
        <p>
          <!--Filler text-->
          The following text consists of a mock Latin which has been
          based uponthe average frequency of characters and word lengths
          of the English language in order to reproduce a reasonably
          accurate overall visual impression. Lorem ipsum dolor sit amet,
          consectetur adipscing elit, sed diam nonnumy eiusmod tempor
          incidunt ut labore et dolore magna aliquam erat volupat.</p>
          <p>Et harumd dereud facilis est er expedit distinct. Nam liber
          a tempor cum soluta nobis eligend optio comque nihil quod a
          impedit anim id quod maxim placeat facer possim omnis es volup-
          tas assumenda est, omnis dolor repellend. Temporem autem quin-
          sud et aur office debit aut tum rerum necesit atib saepe
          eveniet ut er repudiand sint et molestia non este recusand.
          <!--end Filler text-->
        </p>
        <p>
```

```
<!--Filler text-->
The following text consists of a mock Latin which has been based upon
the average frequency of characters and word lengths of the
English language in order to reproduce a reasonably accurate overall
visual impression. Lorem ipsum dolor sit amet, consectetur adipscing
elit, sed diam nonnumy  eiusmod tempor incidunt ut labore et dolore
magna aliquam erat volupat.</p>
<p>Et harumd dereud facilis est er expedit distinct. Nam liber a tem-
por cum soluta nobis eligend optio comque nihil quod a impedit anim
id quod maxim placeat facer possim omnis es voluptas assumenda est,
omnis dolor repellend. Temporem autem quinsud et aur office debit aut
tum rerum necesit atib saepe eveniet ut er repudiand sint et molestia
non este recusand.
        <!--end Filler text-->
    </p>
    ]]></item>
 <item name="head"><![CDATA[{Here Too!}]]></item>
 <item name="Sidebar"><![CDATA[
    <h1>Our Pictures</h1>
    <p><!--Filler text-->
        The following text consists of a mock Latin which has been
        based upon  the average frequency of characters and word
        lengths of the English language in order to reproduce a reason-
        ably accurate overall visual impression. Lorem ipsum dolor sit
        amet, consectetur adipscing elit, sed diam nonnumy eiusmod tem-
        por dmxtemplatum ut labore et dolore magna aliquam erat volu-
        pat.</p>
    <p>Et harumd dereud facilis est er expedit distinct. Nam liber a
        tempor  cum soluta nobis halsteadis optio comque nihil quod a
        impedit anim id quod maxim placeat facer possim omnis es
        voluptas assumenda est, omnis dolor repellend. Temporem autem
        murrayus et aur office debit aut tum rerum necesit atib saepe
        eveniet ut er repudiand sint et molestia non este recusand.
        <!--end Filler text->
    </p>
    ]]></item>
</templateItems>
```

Notice that the bold areas relate directly to an editable region in the template-based file, including template parameters and repeating regions. There is one area shown in the listing that is safe, yet not boldfaced (`<item  name="head"><![CDATA[  ]]></item>`), because that area has no content. This is where you would add JavaScript, page-specific CSS, or page-specific meta tags.

If you're really adventurous, you can even manually specify a different template by editing the line containing /Templates/MX_Templates.dwt, as long as you know which templates are available to choose from within the site.

Hints and Tips

Whenever you modify the site template, it's a good idea to also make the XML file by using the File > Export > Template Data as XML option. That way, your XML source boilerplate stays current and can serve as a backup in the event of catastrophe, which *never* happens to us, of course.

Make sure that you have a backup of your XML source file prior to editing it so that you always have a reference as to how it is supposed to look. It's a good idea to print out a copy or make an XML boilerplate file to toy around with.

Edit only the contents of the CDATA area between the second opening bracket [and the first closing bracket] unless you are adventurous and know XML and your template structure inside and out. An example of an editable CDATA area is highlighted in bold as follows:

```
<![CDATA[ Edit in this area only ]]>
```

You can create this file by hand, but it takes more explanation than the scope of this chapter permits. We recommend the book entitled *Inside Dreamweaver MX* by Laura Gutman et al. (2003, New Riders Publishing) and *eLearning with Dreamweaver MX: Building Online Learning Applications* by Betsy Bruce (2003, New Riders) as excellent references regarding the use and editing of XML files. As long as you follow the "Hints & Tips" section, you'll be fine and on your way with little effort on your part.

Import XML into Template

In our opinion, this DMX function has to be the slickest feature. Having the ability to receive content from a client, add it to the XML boilerplate, and import into the template-based web site with a button click or two is mighty powerful.

This menu option is sometimes used with File > Export > Template Data as XML, with which you create the necessary boilerplate XML file. Unlike Template Data as XML, however, you should reuse this option for each created XML file to create template child pages (see Figure 5.4). In other words, if you have more than one page of content to import into your template-based site, you should create multiple XML files with your content and use this command to import each XML file into the template-structured site.

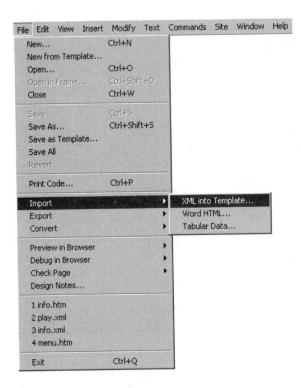

Figure 5.4   Import XML into Template option.

When to Use This Method

Use this method to import data from an XML file into any and all editable regions of a selected template, using one or two mouse clicks.

How to Use This Method

Exercise 5.2:   Import XML into Template

In this exercise, you put all that you have learned about the Import XML into Template option into practical use through a generalized example.

1. It's assumed that you have the required site defined in DMX and Dreamweaver is running. If necessary, please see the instructions in the section "Defining your Site" in the Section I, or start Dreamweaver if your site is already defined.

2. Open a new blank document by using File > New > Basic Page > HTML, select File > Import > XML into Template, and the Import XML dialog should appear, as you see in Figure 5.5.

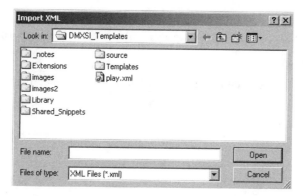

Figure 5.5   Import XML dialog.

Note

You opened a blank document only to activate the option. It has no bearing on importing the XML content into the specified template. No changes will be made to the blank document unless you save the generated file with this filename. You could just as easily use File > New and select a blank html document to perform this exercise.

3. We've taken the liberty of creating an XML file (play.xml) for you to use for the purpose of this exercise. If you choose to use your own file, then have at it; otherwise, select play.xml and click the Open button.

   Dreamweaver MX does its magic, creating a new page based on the template specified in the XML file and inserting the editable region content in the appropriate areas of the template.

   Notice that the blank new document is still open and unmodified, but DMX has created an entirely new untitled document during the process of importing the XML data.

4. Save the new untitled file as **play.htm**, close all open documents, and leave DMX open for the next exercise.

Warnings

Take care when you are editing the generated XML file. The File > Import > XML into Template option will not be at all happy with careless handling, and it will let you know by displaying error messages.

Cloaking

Questions in the Macromedia Dreamweaver and UltraDev support forums often look like these:

> "Why is it that when I PUT a file with its dependent files, the design notes, the templates, and the library items are also PUT? I'm working alone and do not need to share those files."

> "Why is the Templates folder and its files PUT to the server when I PUT other files from my local site? I thought those DWT files had no function on the server!"

Well, Macromedia has listened and responded with a slick solution to those issues by way of its cloaking feature, available in the Site Definition and Site panel (see Figure 5.6).

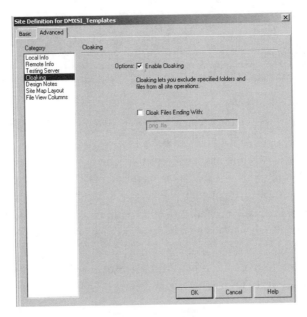

Figure 5.6   The Site Definition dialog, Cloaking category.

The cloaking feature allows you to define folders and files (by extension only) that are hidden from various operations (see Table 5.1). It's very easy to use once you know where to configure everything. The cloaking feature is based on the Site Definition, so fortunately you can make it unique to each site.

Table 5.1   Summary of Cloaking Operations

Site Asset	Excludes Asset From
Templates folder	Get and put *only*
Library folder	Get and put *only*
All other site assets	Put, Get, Check In, Check Out, Reports, Synchronize, Asset panel contents, Select newer local and newer remote, Sitewide operations, such as check and change links and search/replace, and Template & library updating

The most common folders and files that people want to cloak are listed in Table 5.2.

Table 5.2   Summary of Commonly Cloaked Files

Site Elements	Description of Asset
Templates	Folder that holds templates
Library	Folder that holds library items
Source:	Typical folder for source files such as word documents.
.FLA	Flash source files
.PNG	Fireworks source file
.PSD	PhotoShop Source File
.MNO	Macromedia Notes file (used by Dreamweaver for many different things, including Round Trip functionality, Design notes, etc.) Further reading on the _notes folder and .mno files can be found in Chapter 44 of *Inside Dreamweaver MX* (2003, New Riders Publishing).

Access the cloaking configuration by opening the Site Definition dialog and clicking the Advanced tab, and selecting the Cloaking category. Click the Enable Cloaking checkbox to turn the Cloaking feature off and on (the feature is Enabled by default when you create a site). The Cloak Files Ending With checkbox enables the files specified in the list field to be cloaked site-wide, not by folder (by default, this option is disabled when you create a site).

Exercise 5.3:   Cloaking Files and Folders

In this exercise, you put all that you have learned about cloaking into practical use through a generalized example. You will learn how to cloak the following items: a folder, a group of folders, and a specific file extension. You also learn how to use the Uncloak and Uncloak All features.

   1. Make sure that you have the required site defined in DMX and that Dreamweaver is running. See "Defining Your Site" in Section I if you need to review the steps, or start Dreamweaver if your site is already defined.

2. You can access the related Cloaking menu system two different ways. The first method is to click the Site button in the Site panel (top right) or in the Site menu option on the Macintosh; the second is to use the Site panel context menu (right-clicking, or Ctrl+click, in the Site panel file/folder listing area). For the purposes of our demonstration, expand the source folder by double-clicking it, or click the plus (+) button beside it. You should now see something similar to Figure 5.7.

3. Select the Site drop-down on the Site panel. This should bring up the Site menu. Select Cloaking and verify that there is a checkmark beside Enable Cloaking (this is enabled by default when you create the Site Definition). If there is no checkmark beside Enable Cloaking, select that menu option or click the Setting menu item. (Now we can kill two birds with one stone.) By selecting the Settings menu item, you open the Site Definition dialog to the Cloaking category, where you place a checkmark in both check boxes and enter .PNG as the file type to cloak. Click OK. After you click OK, Dreamweaver tells you that the site cache has to be re-created. Click OK, and you should now see something similar to Figure 5.8.

Note

Your site cache was rebuilt for DMX to track the change in configuration.

Make sure that any .PNG files in the site (only in the source folder for this example) have a red diagonal line running through them. This is your visual reminder that the files or folders are cloaked from the operations specified in Table 5.1.

4. In the Site panel, click the folder named Templates, and then click the Site button. In the menu that appears, select Cloaking, and then Cloak. Because we are using the Template folder as an example, a warning message is displayed (see Figure 5.9). Click OK. You should now see something similar to Figure 5.10.

Note

Notice that there is no requirement to re-create the cache because DMX is dealing with a folder and doesn't have to search the entire Site Definition to mark files.

5. Repeat step 4, using the images folder. You should then have the Templates and images folder cloaked as well as two PNG files in the source folder. If this is not what you see, repeat steps 2 through 5 until you've cloaked the right files.

6. Realizing that a mistake was made (we don't want the images folder cloaked), select the images folder, right-click (Ctrl+click) to bring up the context menu, select Cloaking, and then Uncloak. This will uncloak the images folder so that it and the files inside are available to all DMX operations.

Figure 5.7
The Site panel with the source folder
expanded (before file cloaking is enabled).

Figure 5.8
The Site panel with the source folder expanded
(after file cloaking is enabled).

Figure 5.9   Template/Library warning message.

7. Now suppose that you've decided it's a good idea to put all files to the server. Click the right mouse button (Ctrl+click) to bring up the context menu. Select Cloaking and Uncloak All, which will remove all cloaking from your site. DMX displays a warning dialog stating: `Uncloak All will cause all of your cloaked items for this site to be uncloaked. Are you sure you wish to do this?` Clicking No will cancel the operation. Clicking Yes will remove all folder cloaking and change the site preferences in the Cloaking category to disable file cloaking and then remove all individual file cloaks that may exist in the site. The site cache is re-created and the Site panel is repopulated with the changes.

 Note

You can temporarily disable cloaking by turning it off in the site preferences. When you re-enable it, previously cloaked files/folders are retained and will be displayed as cloaked.

Figure 5.10
The Site panel with the Templates folder cloaked.

Using JavaScript That References URLs and Images, SSIs, and SWFs in Templates and Library Items

One of the great advantages of DWX is that once a file is saved within the site (and its links are cached), DWX can then manage all the dependent links in the file—adjusting the links as necessary as files are moved within the site. Templates, however, can have problems with links mentioned in SSIs, SWFs, and JavaScript (especially when images or URLs are referenced in the JavaScript). Following are some suggestions for using these items with templates:

- *Always* use absolute links (`http://www.domain.com/folder/file.htm`) or root relative links (`/folder/file.htm`) to images, objects, and URLs. Of course, if the target file is moved, DWX will still fail to update the absolute link. This method protects you only when the document containing the link is moved.

Note

When using root-relative links, you must ensure that the objects you linked to in this manner are part of the current Site Definition. Using this method with objects outside the Site Definition will not bring them into the current Site Definition and will result in broken links or create functionality issues with the page.

- Remember, however, that the referenced source items *must* be uploaded to your server and you must be connected to the Internet in order for local browser previews to be visible and functional. Remote files such as these (http links) are not seen in Dreamweaver Design view.

- In these specific instances, *never* use document relative links or they will break when you create a template child page.

- In the case of JavaScript, using an external JavaScript source file instead of page-coded JavaScript seems to overcome several issues. For best results, use the first method listed in combination with this point.

Summary

In addition to detaching pages from templates, Dreamweaver gives you the ability to attach different templates to the same document (although not two at the same time!). Although there are stringent limitations to this function, it does have a place and is a valuable function when you use it with the limitations in mind. You also have learned how to Export your Template Editable region structure to an XML file and to manipulate that XML file for fast transformation of existing content into your template-based site.

Finally, the ability to cloak files and folders from the various Dreamweaver MX operations is a very big bonus that we thank Macromedia for. Sometimes this is a very useful feature and other times you may have no use for it at all, but at least now the option is available to you.

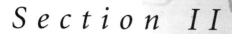

Section II

The Project

Before proceeding with this section of the
book, we strongly encourage you to read
Section I, "Reusable Page Elements," where
we cover in detail all aspects of templates,
library items, and snippets. You need to

have a basic understanding of Dreamweaver's reusable elements so that you can use them in building the project in this part of the book.

In this section, you create a project, based on what you learned in Section I of this book. The project you'll be creating is a web site for a fictitious company named Hot Cool Toys. As you work through the following chapters, you will build the site based on DMX's templates, library items, and snippets. The exercises in these chapters showcase the various capabilities of those elements. It is the versatility of these tools that enables you to easily adapt a complex site to different page layout needs, and then easily maintain the site after production.

All of the files you will need to complete this project are available on the support site, www.dreamweavermx-templates.com/register.cfm, including PNG graphics and template files. You also will find other files there, representing intermediate steps in the construction of the template pages. Reference will be made to these intermediate files throughout the following narrative.

The following discussion focuses more on the utility of the different template regions than on elements of page layout or design. A base page layout already will be in place, and each variable area of the page will be brought under the control of a master template page.

In many cases, we will work "outside" DMX's user interface for these regions. This is not done lightly, but rather because the interface sometimes does not allow the full power of these new regions to be exploited. If you are feeling queasy about getting your hands into the code, you'd better get the Dramamine ready!

Note

Often when we recommend this "manual" approach to the project, we do so for a specific reason, which will be pointed out either in the text or in a nearby note.

Defining the Site

The examples in this section are cumulative, which means that each step proceeds logically from the previous completed steps. Accordingly, please configure your Hot Cool Toys Project Site Definition as detailed here:

1. Download the file named HotCoolToys.zip from www.dreamweavermx-templates.com/register.cfm.

2. After the file is downloaded, extract the zip file to a folder of your choosing. Again, you can put this folder anywhere on your hard drive—just make sure that you remember its name and location! Be sure the extraction process retains folder information so that all the links work properly. (You can use an archiving utility such as WinZip or StuffIt to extract the file.)

3. Name the new folder you created **HotCoolToys**. This will become the root folder of your project site.

4. Start DMX and configure a new local site as follows:

   - Select Site > New Site.

   - Click the Advanced tab and complete the fields as outlined here:

     Site Name: HotCoolToys

     Local Root Folder: Browse to and select the HotCoolToys folder you created to hold the extracted files. On the PC, this might be C:\HotCoolToys\ and on the Mac this might be OSX_Drive:Library:Sites:HotCoolToys.

     Default Images Folder: HotCoolToys\images\ (or HotCoolToys:images:)

   - Leave the remainder of the settings at their defaults.

   - Click OK to save the site definition and close the Site Definition dialog box.

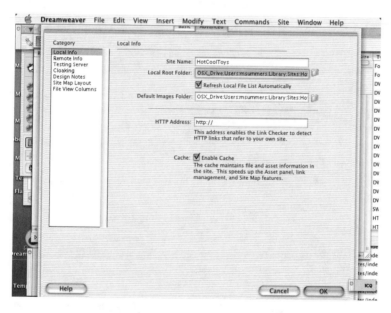

Figure S2.1   The completed HotCoolToys site definition.

5. Make sure that the site named HotCoolToys is selected in the Site panel. If there are no files or folders showing in the local site view, click the plus (+) sign beside the site name to expand the site files.

Now proceed with the remaining steps of the project in the chapter exercises. ■

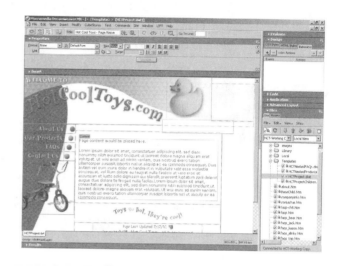

Chapter 6

Building the Hot Cool Toys Base Template

With any web site project, the early decisions are the most important because they determine the methods and strategies you use from that point forward. For that reason, it is worthwhile to take a minute and examine the site's structure and general layout plan.

The structure of the Hot Cool Toys site is a very simple tree. The single home page will have branches to each subsection page. As you navigate through the site, a variety of graphic clues show your location within the site. DMX's new template functionality allows you to construct a single-base template that contains the logic for those changes to occur.

Warning

When you are using template parameters and expressions, you can no longer reliably preview the template (F12 or Shift+F12) because the template routines that depend on parameter values have not yet run to produce the complete code for the page. In our case, previewing a template containing these types of logical constructions caused an `Unterminated String Constant` Runtime error to pop up). To preview your work and avoid these runtime browser errors, you must create a child page, set parameters, and then preview the child page.

Examining the Project's Layout

Let's start by taking a look at the desired page appearance. Figure 6.1 shows the general layout plan for the Hot Cool Toys web site.

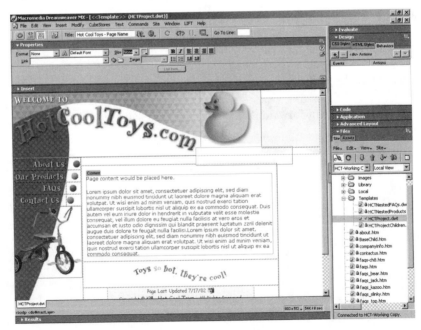

Figure 6.1   HCT site layout plan.

1. The Welcome Message appears only on the first page.

2. The Masthead Graphic is different on the first page, but is the same on each interior page.

3. The Masthead Toy is different on each section's pages, including the home page.

4. The Section Name is different for each section, but does not appear on the home page.

5. The Navigation Toy is different on the first page but is the same on each interior page.

6. The HTML Title is different on each page.

7. The `down-state` navigation button is different on each page.

Clearly, you need a way to tell DMX the name for each child page. With this information, DMX can then make all the rest of the decisions about which graphics to use and where to use them. But let's start simply by first adding a template parameter to the page, and then using it to set the page's title.

Before starting anything, make sure that you have defined your site properly, as specified in the Section II introduction.

Examining the Site

Use DMX to open this site, and browse to the `Templates` folder and open the template file named `HCTProject.dwt`.

Take a moment to cruise around the site. Note that there are subfolders under the `images` folder, one for each section; that is, `about`, `contact us`, `faqs`, and so on. The images relevant to each section of the site are in these subfolders, with two exceptions:

- Navigation button images are contained in the navigation subfolder.

- Non-specific or common images are in the root of the images folder.

The Page Title

Fasten your seatbelts and get your keyboards lubed, 'cause we're going in. We will start at the top of the page and work our way down, proceeding in a systematic way to manage each of the page's variable regions.

Exercise 6.1:   Setting the Page Title

You learned in Chapter 3, "All About Templates and Regions," that inserting an optional region on the page will add a comment line specifying the optional region's name as a template parameter. Unfortunately, when you use DMX's Insert > Template Objects > Optional Region command, several things happen in the document:

1. A template parameter comment is inserted in the head of the document (this is good):

   ```
   <!-- TemplateParam name="page_name" type="boolean" value="true" -->
   ```

2. This template parameter is *always* inserted as a Boolean type parameter (this is not necessarily good).

3. Depending on the location of your cursor in the document at the moment when you initiate the insertion, the following code is inserted in the document (this is bad):

   ```
   <!-- TemplateBeginIf cond="page_name" —>page_name<!--
   TemplateEndIf -->
   ```

In this case, we need for #1 to happen so that we can define the template parameter that will be used in the page title, but we need that parameter to be a text type parameter, not a Boolean. And we certainly don't need the `BeginIf` condition inserted in the body. So, we'll make some adjustments:

1. Open `HCTProject.dwt`.

2. Select anything in the Design View window and select Insert > Template Objects > Optional Region. Name the region **"page_name"**. Click OK to close the dialog box. Then, in Code View, edit the comment in the document's head (referenced in #1) to look like this:

   ```
   <!-- TemplateParam name="page_name" type="text" value="Home" -->
   ```

   This makes sure that any child page will carry this (editable) parameter with the value of `"Home"`. This takes care of items #1 and #2.

3. Using Code View to find the conditional `if` comment in the body of the page (remember what was selected when you applied the snippet?) and delete it completely (by removing both `<!-- TemplateBeginIf cond="page_name" -->` and `<!-- TemplateEndIf -->`) so that the end result is a page with a single new comment line on it. Depending on the position of your cursor when you insert this snippet, you may find that this snippet is appended at the end of existing content in the head editable region, which is not a problem:

   ```
   <!-- TemplateParam name="page_name" type="text" value="Home" -->
   ```

Note

You could have achieved the same result by positioning the cursor anywhere in the head of the page's code, selecting Templates > Parameters > Text Snippet, and editing the name and value attributes as shown previously. Because this is easier when you are using snippets, we will concentrate on this method throughout the remainder of this project.

4. Now for the fun part. We will use a template expression for the page title, like this:

`<title>Hot Cool Toys - @@(page_name)@@</title>`

Make that change in the page's `<title>` code in Code View or in the Title field in either view, and save the template as `HCTProject1.dwt`. Next, spawn a child page from it (use methods already described in earlier chapters to spawn a child page).

5. Save the child page as `HCTProject2.html`. You should see something that looks like Figure 6.2.

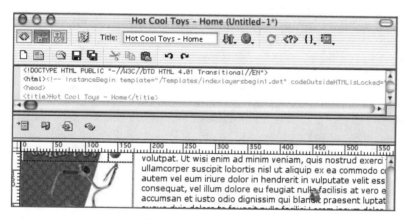

Figure 6.2   Using a template expression to set the child page's title.

Note that the child page already displays Home in the title bar because you gave the template parameter the value of `"Home"` as a default value.

6. With this child page still open, select Modify > Template Properties and change page_name to `"Contact Us"`. When you click OK, the name on the title bar immediately changes to Contact Us.

7. Save and close this child page.

The Masthead

You're off to a good start. You have a page that automatically uses the page_name parameter to set the title. Because you need to change the parameter value for each child page manually, however, this is no better than manually changing the title. We can make it better.

Exercise 6.2:   Managing the Masthead

As specified earlier, the masthead image needs to be unique on the site's homepage while using a different unique image for the remainder of the site pages. Here's how to do this:

1. Open `HCTProject1.dwt` and your Layers panel (F2), and select the layer called `mastLayer` by clicking it in the Layers panel.

2. Select the image contained within the layer (`masthead.jpg`), and select Modify > Templates > Make Attribute Editable. In the ensuing dialog, enable the `src` attribute as editable, assign it a label of `masthead`, select the type URL, and enter a default value of `../images/masthead.jpg` if it isn't already populated with this value, as shown in Figure 6.3.

> **Note**
>
> Because you will be manually entering links for the image files in this project, you need to be careful to enter these links with the correct "relativity." Normally, when you use DMX's UI to browse to linked files, these links are entered relative to the TEMPLATE page, and then adjusted by DMX when the child page is spawned to reflect the final location of the child page in the site's folder hierarchy. When you are using template expressions to contain links to files, however, this adjustment will *not* be done at the time the child page is spawned. This means that you must be careful to enter such links (in expressions) as relative to the final location of the page. In the case of the HCT Project, this is a simple matter because all of the site's pages are at the root level of the site. Other sites may be more challenging to manage manually using this method. To overcome this limitation, we recommend using site root relative links to URLs and images.

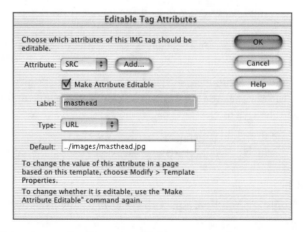

Figure 6.3   Giving the mastheadImage an editable source attribute.

Click OK to save the changes and close the Editable Tag Attributes dialog.

3. Save this file as `HCTProject2.dwt`.

4. Spawn a child page (as already described), and note that its Masthead graphic and title are consistent with the Home page. Next you need to change things a bit, so save this file as `HCTProject3.html`.

Note

Having made this tag editable, you will now see that the graphic becomes a placeholder instead of the actual graphic image that you saw previously. Don't worry about this!

5. After you've saved the new child page, select Modify > Template Properties > and change `masthead` from this:

   `images/masthead.jpg`

   to this:

   `images/masthead2.jpg`

   Also, change `page_name` from `"Home"` to `"About Us"`. Click OK to close the Template Properties dialog box.

Note

We use `images/masthead2.jpg` to point at the generic interior masthead graphic that is located in the root images folder.

6. It's like magic! The masthead graphic becomes the interior graphic, and the page's title changes to `"Hot Cool Toys - About Us"`! Save this page as `HCTProject3.html`.

Note

Although incredibly cool, this method has a problem. Because we created `masthead` (the template parameter) as a URL type parameter, DMX will track the link to the graphic element it specifies in the *child* page, but not in the template page. This means that if `images/masthead.jpg` is moved or renamed, DMX will adjust that link in all existing child pages, but it *will not* adjust the link in the template itself, which translates into a broken image in any new child pages that you create! Bummer. You will just have to do that yourself. The same comment applies to links specified in your template expressions, too.

Note

You could have achieved the same result with a completely manual approach by inserting a URL snippet into the starting page, adjusting the name and the value attributes of the snippet, and editing the image source statement to replace the existing `mastheadImage` pathname with the template expression —`@@(masthead)@@`. As far as DMX is concerned, the pages produced would be identical either way.

Note

Using a template expression/editable attribute for an image source statement prevents the image from being shown in the Template page's Design View at all. Do not be concerned that HCTProject2.dwt shows only an image placeholder for mastheadImage. All this will come out in the wash, because DMX does not do real-time evaluation of the template expressions in template documents! This expression will be evaluated only when the template program is run; that is, when a child page is spawned (created), a template parameter is changed in the child page, or the child page is saved.

The Masthead Toy

We have three of the seven variable areas taken care of now (remember that two of the variable areas were welcome message and masthead graphic, both of which were managed with the interchange of a single masthead image).

Exercise 6.3:   Managing the Masthead Toy

Let's turn to the masthead toy image. The masthead toy image needs to be unique on each of the site's pages. Here are the steps:

1. Open HCTProject2.dwt.

2. Click the mastheadtoyImage and note that it is contained in masttoyLayer. Although you could simply make the src attribute of the masheadtoyImage editable (like you did with the mastheadImage graphic), it would require that you remember to make the edit and change the graphic. Because you have already defined a template parameter called page_name, you could just insert an image based on the value of page_name! That seems like a smart way to handle this variable area, and it can be done pretty easily with a MultipleIf conditional region.

3. Open the Snippets panel and locate the snippet called M_Block Text (make sure your Snippets Name field is expanded sufficiently to show the entire name).

4. Select mastheadtoyImage in HCTProject2.dwt and insert the snippet you just located. You have now made a mess (see Figure 6.4), but don't worry. We'll fix it.

5. Now for some trickery. In Code View, change this line:

```
<!-- TemplateBeginIfClause cond="" --> Insert Output 1
<!-- TemplateEndIfClause -->
```

to this:

```
<!-- TemplateBeginIfClause cond="page_name=='Home'" -->
<img src="../images/masthead_toy.jpg" name="mastheadtoyImage"
width="153"
height="159" id="mastheadtoyImage"><!-- TemplateEndIfClause -->
```

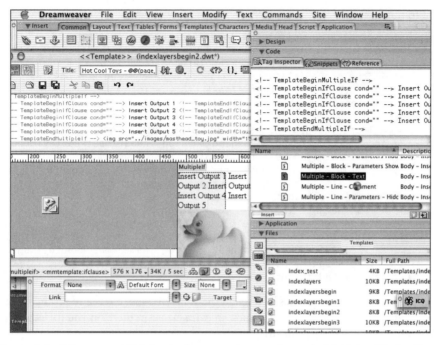

Figure 6.4   What a mess! This is what happens when you insert the Multiple – Block – Text snippet.

> **Note**
> We have used a link relative to the template file because this link will be adjusted by the template program when the child page is spawned. Such links specified within template optional regions will fall within the control of the template program and be adjusted appropriately.

This line causes the template to evaluate the parameter named `'page_name'`. If it finds the value `"Home"`, it will write the image tag as shown. If it does not, the template will proceed to the next clause of the `MultipleIf` until it finds a match. If no match is found, nothing is displayed.

6. To complete the `MultipleIf`, change these lines:

```
  <!-- TemplateBeginIfClause cond="" --> Insert Output 2
<!-- TemplateEndIfClause -->
  <!-- TemplateBeginIfClause cond="" --> Insert Output 3
<!-- TemplateEndIfClause -->
  <!-- TemplateBeginIfClause cond="" --> Insert Output 4
<!-- TemplateEndIfClause -->
  <!-- TemplateBeginIfClause cond="" --> Insert Output 5
<!-- TemplateEndIfClause -->
```

to this:

```
   <!-- TemplateBeginIfClause cond="page_name=='About Us'" -->
<img src="../images/about/masthead_toy.jpg" name="mastheadtoyImage"
width="153" height="159"><!— TemplateEndIfClause -->
   <!-- TemplateBeginIfClause cond="page_name=='Contact Us'" -->
<img src="../images/contactus/masthead_toy.jpg"
name="mastheadtoyImage"
width="153" height="159"><!— TemplateEndIfClause -->
   <!-- TemplateBeginIfClause cond="page_name=='FAQs'" -->
<img src="../images/faqs/masthead_toy.jpg" name="mastheadtoyImage"
width="153" height="159"><!— TemplateEndIfClause -->
   <!-- TemplateBeginIfClause cond="page_name=='Our Products'" -->
<img src="../images/products/masthead_toy.jpg"
name="mastheadtoyImage"
width="153" height="159"><!— TemplateEndIfClause -->
   <!-- TemplateBeginIfClause cond="page_name=='Company
   Information'" -->
<img src="../images/info/masthead_toy.jpg" name="mastheadtoyImage"
width="153" height="159">
<!-- TemplateEndIfClause -->
```

so that we perform a series of tests on the value of page_name, and set the image used for each such value. (We snuck an extra clause in there on you to accommodate the Company Information page!)

7. Finally, make sure that you have deleted the original image reference from the code by changing this:

```
<!-- TemplateEndMultipleIf --> <img src="../images/masthead_toy.jpg"
name="mastheadtoyImage" width="153" height="159"></div>
```

to this:

```
<!-- TemplateEndMultipleIf --></div>
```

8. Does it look like we have fixed the mess? Not exactly, because Design View will now show *each* image explicitly on the page (the references are there in the code—they have to be shown). But watch this: Save the file as HCTProject3.dwt and spawn a child from it. Hmmm—not bad.

9. Save this child file as HCTProject4.html, and use the familiar Modify > Template Properties command to set two parameters: Set page_name to "Our Products" and masthead to images/masthead2.jpg.

   Ta-DAA! No mess.

10. Save the template (HCTProject3.dwt), update the child page (HCTProject4.html), and then close the child page. Leave the template open for further editing.

> **Note**
>
> We could have used any value for page_name within the range of pages in the site. Because there is no error-checking in this logic, using an unrecognized value for page_name will simply produce an empty layer! Ideally, such logical constructs should contain error-checking routines as well.
>
> In fact, you can easily add this error-checking in the following way. Add another clause to the MultipleIf tests in HCTProject3.dwt, as follows:
>
> ```
>     <!-- TemplateBeginIfClause cond="page_name!='Company
> Information'" --><span class="error">Please
>     Enter A Valid Page Name (Home, About Us, Contact Us, FAQs, Our
> Products, Company Information)!</span><!-- TemplateEndIfClause -->
> ```
>
> This takes advantage of the fact that a multipleIf construction will stop executing as soon as a true condition is encountered. The last clause will be executed only if all the previous tests have failed.

The Section Name Variable Area

We have three more effects to go, so let's hurry on with the section name variable area. You can take care of this effect the same way you did for the masthead graphic or for the mastheadtoy. But let's add another level of complexity to things.

Exercise 6.4:   Managing the Section Name

This time, you will create a URL parameter for the section name image and write some logic that will change the value of that parameter based on the page_name parameter's value.

1. Open HCTProject3.dwt.

2. Position the cursor in the head of the document, using Code View, just below this line:

   ```
   <!-- TemplateParam name="masthead" type="URL"
   value="../images/masthead.jpg" -->
   ```

   Now insert a "URL" parameter snippet, edit the name to "sectionimage", and change the value to "../images/shim.gif", like this:

   ```
   <!-- TemplateParam name="sectionimage" type="URL"
   value="../images/shim.gif" -->
   ```

3. Directly beneath the opening body tag <body>, add a "M_Block Parameters Hidden" snippet, which will add this code:

   ```
   <!-- TemplateBeginMultipleIf -->
   <!-- TemplateBeginIfClause cond="" --> <!-- @@("")@@ -->
   <!-- TemplateEndIfClause -->
   <!-- TemplateBeginIfClause cond="" --> <!-- @@("")@@ -->
   ```

```
<!-- TemplateEndIfClause -->
<!-- TemplateBeginIfClause cond="" --> <!-- @@("")@@ -->
<!-- TemplateEndIfClause -->
<!-- TemplateBeginIfClause cond="" --> <!-- @@("")@@ -->
<!-- TemplateEndIfClause -->
<!-- TemplateBeginIfClause cond="" --> <!-- @@("")@@ -->
<!-- TemplateEndIfClause -->
<!-- TemplateEndMultipleIf -->
```

Note

You can put this MultipleIf conditional code anywhere in the body section of the page and it will still run just fine. For convenience of code lookup, we have placed it directly under the body tag.

There are a couple of things you need to know about this beast. The first is that because you have already assigned to the sectionimage parameter a URL pointing at shim.gif, and because the Home page does not display a section name graphic, you do not need to test for the home page in a page_name test. The template program will put the transparent GIF in place and no image will appear as a result. The second is that because you are defining "template logic" with ASCII text characters that you do not want to appear on-screen, you need to put the logic within an HTML comment to make it invisible—that's why the expression in each separate MultipleIf clause is wrapped in comment tags.

4. Make the condition of the first clause test the value of the page_name parameter, like this:

```
cond="page_name=='About Us'"
```

If this condition is true (we have used the comparison operator == here), the expression that follows it will be evaluated when the child page is spawned. You need to make that expression actually set the value of the sectionimage parameter to the appropriate image's URL, as follows:

```
<!-- @@(sectionimage='images/about/sectionname.gif')@@ -->
```

Note

Because this reference to the sectionname.gif image falls within a template expression statement, you must be careful to make it relative to the final location of the child page, not the parent template page.

In other words, if the page name is About Us, set the sectionimage parameter so that it points at the sectionname.gif image that is in the about image folder (we have used the assignment operator = here).

5. Change the remaining parts of this `MultipleIf` snippet as follows:

```
<!-- TemplateBeginIfClause cond="page_name=='Home'" -->
<!-- @@(sectionimage='images/shim.gif')@@ -->
<!-- TemplateEndIfClause -->
<!-- TemplateBeginIfClause cond="page_name=='Our Products'" -->
<!-- @@(sectionimage='images/products/sectionname.gif')@@ -->
<!-- TemplateEndIfClause -->
<!-- TemplateBeginIfClause cond="page_name=='Contact Us'" -->
<!-- @@(sectionimage='images/contactus/sectionname.gif')@@ -->
<!-- TemplateEndIfClause -->
<!-- TemplateBeginIfClause cond="page_name=='FAQs'" -->
<!-- @@(sectionimage='images/faqs/sectionname.gif')@@ -->
<!-- TemplateEndIfClause -->
<!-- TemplateBeginIfClause cond="page_name=='Company
Information'" -->
<!-- @@(sectionimage='images/info/sectionname.gif')@@ -->
<!-- TemplateEndIfClause -->
```

Each clause tests the page_name parameter and then adjusts the path to `sectionname.gif` accordingly.

6. As before, you will add a final clause to the `MultipleIf` for some error checking:

```
<!-- TemplateBeginIfClause cond="page_name!='
Company Information'" -->
<!-- @@(sectionimage='images/shim.gif')@@ -->
<!-- TemplateEndIfClause -->
```

Note

We could have used the same error message as before, but the error messages would overwrite each other and make it hard to read. The easiest solution is to use the shim image on error for this `MultipleIf` conditional region because its only purpose is to set a parameter value for `sectionimage`.

Place this clause just above the closing:

```
<!-- TemplateEndMultipleIf -->
```

7. To finish things up, find the layer called `sectionnameLayer` and change the contained image tag from this:

```
<img src="../images/shim.gif" name="sectionnameImage" width="244"
height="43 id="sectionnameImage ">
```

to this:

```
<img src="@@(sectionimage)@@" name="sectionnameImage" width="244"
height="43" id="sectionnameImage">
```

This directs the template to evaluate the `sectionimage` parameter and place its value in the `src` attribute.

8. Save the template page as HCTProject4.dwt and use it to spawn a new child page.

9. Save the child as HCTProject5.html, and then use Modify > Template Properties to specify page_name of "Our Products" and masthead of "images/mast-head2.jpg". Click OK to apply the changes.

When you save this child page again, you will see the effect of the logic you just added.

The Navigation Buttons and Toy Image

We have saved one of the best features for nearly last, so (drum roll) here's "else"! Get a strong cup of coffee and have a comfortable seat.

Exercise 6.5:   Managing the Navigation Buttons

A good place to use this logic is setting the down state of the navigation button so that it is consistent with the section name image; for example, showing the FAQ button in a down state on the FAQs page.

1. Open HCTProject4.dwt.

2. Select the "About Us" button and display Code View. Select everything from <img src="../images through _butt"> and copy it to the clipboard using Ctrl+C (Command+C) so that this code is waiting to be pasted back when you need it:

```
<img  src="../images/navigation/aboutus.gif"  name="aboutus_butt"
width="135" height="20" vspace="5" border="0" id="aboutus_butt">
```

3. Now, still in Code View, click just to the left of <a href and insert the following template expression fragment:

```
@@(page_name=="About Us" ? '
```

You are inserting logic here that says to test the value of the template parameter called "page_name" and if that value is "About Us", then something should be output to the page. What will be output? Why, the contents of the clipboard, of course (with slight modification).

4. Press Ctrl+V (Command+V) or click the Paste icon to paste the clipboard's contents to the page and press the ' key to close the "then" segment of the expression. You should now see this:

```
@@(page_name=="About Us" ? '<img src="../images/navigation/
aboutus.gif" name="aboutus_butt" width="135" height="20"
vspace="5" border="0" id="aboutus_butt">'
```

This is almost exactly what you want. But remember that you must make the link to any other file relative to the final document's location. You don't use the template's location because these expressions are evaluated only at the time you spawn a child page. So change this:

```
<img src="../images
```

to this:

```
<img src="images
```

This ensures that the link will work properly.

The logic you are building will express the following:

If `page_name` is `"About Us"`, then use the `aboutus` `"over"` button state with *no* link, and if the page is not `"About Us"`, then use the regular button with a link to the correct page.

Using template expressions, you can build such logic using the syntax you have begun to implement. The condition part is clear (`page_name="About Us"`); next comes the `{what to do if true}` part of the expression (that's what you are working on now), and then comes the `{what to do if false}` part of the expression, and that's what you will work on soon. To make a final adjustment to the part that you have constructed, you must change the `<img>` tag to specify the over state of the button, so change this:

```
navigation/aboutus.gif"
```

to this:

```
navigation/aboutus_over.gif"
```

This completes the "true" part of the expression. At this point, your code should resemble Figure 6.5.

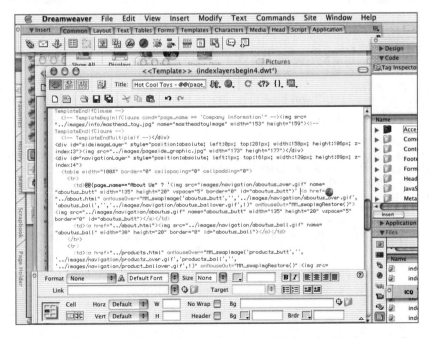

Figure 6.5 The beginning of a complex template expression for selecting the correct button state.

To get ready for the "false" part of the expression, with the cursor positioned as shown earlier in Code View (just to the left of the <a href=), enter the following four characters:

```
{space}:{space}'
```

This code is used to separate the "true" from the "false" (that's the colon character, :) and to begin the part that will be output if the condition is false (that's the single prime character, ').

Now this next part is tricky because you have to worry about properly nested quotation characters. On the same line, find:

```
MM_swapImage(
```

And just after the opening parenthesis of that JavaScript call, type the following five characters (counting spaces):

```
'{space}+{space}"
```

The plus symbol (+) is a JavaScript concatenation that will be used to build an output string for this part of the expression. Now continue through this part of the Code View, and find the event handler:

```
onMouseOut="MM_swap…
```

Enter the following five characters immediately *before* that event handler (onMouseOut):

```
+{space}'"{space}
```

Finally, just to the right of </a>, enter these four characters:

```
')@@
```

Whew! That was hard. If you have been able to follow this explanation, your resulting code should look like this:

```
<td>@@(page_name=="About Us" ? '<img
src="images/navigation/aboutus_over.gif" name="aboutus_butt" width="135"
height="20" vspace="5" border="0" id="aboutus_butt">' : '<a
href="../about.html" onMouseOver="MM_swapImage(' +
"'aboutus_butt','','../images/navigation/aboutus_over.gif','aboutus_ball
','','../images/navigation/aboutus_ballover.gif',1)" + '"
onMouseOut="MM_swapImgRestore()"><img src="../images/navigation/
aboutus.gif" name="aboutus_butt" width="135" height="20" vspace="5"
border="0" id="aboutus_butt"></a>')@@</td>
```

This is a long template expression, but it's one that will get the job done (note that we have included the opening and closing <td> tags for clarity).

5. Now you have a tiny bit of cleanup to make this code work properly in the template's child pages. This is much the same cleanup you did to the "true" part of the expression; that is, change the links to reflect the location of the child page, not the template. This cleanup produces the following code (see Figure 6.6):

```
<td>@@(page_name=="About Us" ? '<img src="images/navigation/
aboutus_over.gif" name="aboutus_butt" width="135" height="20"
vspace="5" border="0" id="aboutus_butt">' : '<a href="about.html"
onMouseOver="MM_swapImage(' + "'aboutus_butt','','images/
navigation/aboutus_over.gif','aboutus_ball','','images/
navigation/aboutus_ballover.gif',1)" + '" onMouseOut=
"MM_swapImgRestore()"><img src="images/navigation/aboutus.gif"
name="aboutus_butt" width="135" height="20" vspace="5" border="0"
id="aboutus_butt"></a>')@@</td>
```

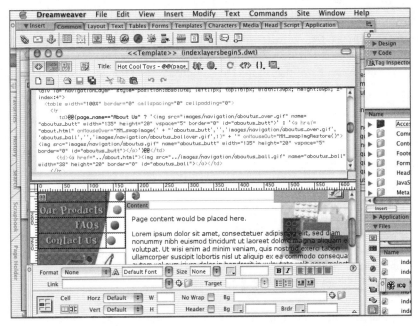

Figure 6.6   Finishing a complex template expression for selecting the correct button state.

> **Note**
>
> The template expression is displayed in the Design View window as "@@".

6. Save this page as `HCTProject5.dwt`, and then spawn a child page.

7. Save the child page as `HCTProject6.html`, and then use Modify > Template Parameters to set the value of page_name to "About Us". Preview the page. Do you see the `aboutus_over.gif` image for the button? Is the link on that button gone? Cool!

8. With `HCTProject6.html` still open, use Modify > Template Parameters again and set `page_name` to `"Contact Us"`. Preview the page. Do you see the normal button image for About Us, and is it linked to the About Us page? If this is not what you see, then please go back through the exercise carefully. If it is what you see, then *Yahoo!*

Each subsequent button can be treated in the same fashion. We will not go through the details of doing this but will leave it as an exercise for you. (I've been waiting all my life to say that in print!) And while you're at it, could you make the same kind of construction to manage the navigation "balls," too?

Exercise 6.6:   Managing the Navigation Toy

The last thing you need to do here is to fix the Navigation Toy image. This one should be a piece of cake for you, given what you already know. You do it with a simple template expression, and it will work by testing the value of `page_name` yet again. If it finds `"Home"`, it will source that image to the trike, and if it doesn't, it will source the image to the duck.

Here's the expression that will make that happen:

```
@@(page_name=="Home" ? '<img src="images/pageside_graphic.jpg"
width="173" height="177">' : '<img src="images/pageside_graphic2.jpg"
width="173" height="177">')@@
```

By now you should be able to inspect that line, know whether it's correct, and know where to put it in the page's code. But just to be sure, we'll tell you:

1. Put it in `HCTProject5.dwt` right here:

   ```
   <div id="navigationimageLayer" style="position:absolute; left:0px;
   top:281px; width:158px; height:106px; z-index:3"><img
   src="../images/pageside_graphic.jpg" width="173"
   height="177"></div>
   ```

   Replace the code beginning with `<img` and ending with `id="sidetoyImage">`.

2. Save this template again, and it will update `HCTProject6.html`.

3. Preview `HCTProject6.html` and set `page_name` first to `"Home"` and then to `"About Us"` to demonstrate that all is working as expected!

Putting It All Together

That has been quite a slog. Thank you for staying with us through it! But we would be remiss if we just left you here, so let's take a minute to clean things up a bit.

Exercise 6.7:   Consolidating Things

Spawning the child pages is still a drag, because you must change multiple parameters each time you do so. You already have a page_name parameter that is doing yeoman work for you—why not just make it do *everything*? Well, you could do just that.

1. Open HCTProject5.dwt and focus your attention on the method you used to manage the masthead image. In fact, you can manage this image in precisely the same way that you have managed the Navigation Toy image— with a template expression and an either/or situation.

    Select the masthead image to position your cursor properly in Code View, and then locate this line of code:

    ```
    <div id="mastLayer" style="position:absolute; left:0px; top:0px;
    width:257px; z-index:1; visibility: visible;"><img
    src="../images/masthead.jpg" name="mastheadImage" width="484"
    height="159" id="mastheadImage"></div>
    ```

    Just a simple change will do, and you will copy it from the Navigation Toy code. Make this line of code now read as follows:

    ```
    <div id="mastLayer" style="position:absolute; left:0px; top:0px;
    width:257px; z-index:1; visibility: visible;">@@(page_name=="Home"
    ? '<img src="images/masthead.jpg" width="484" height="159"
    name="mastheadImage" id="mastheadImage">' : '<img src="images/
    masthead2.jpg" width="484" height="159" name="mastheadImage"
    id="mastheadImage">')@@</div>
    ```

2. Save your template as HCTProject6.dwt, spawn a new page, and save it as HCTProject7.html. Verify that you need to change only the page_name parameter to make everything happen.

Note

Regardless of what you provide as values for masthead and sectionimage, the proper values are converted and used in the child pages.

Summary

This is a complicated chapter because we explored so many new methods. To pull things together, here is a summary of what has been done:

- A template expression based on the value of the parameter "page_name" automatically sets each page's title.

- An editable tag attribute is used for the masthead image so that the masthead graphic on interior pages can be made different from that shown on the home page.

- A `MultipleIf` condition snippet is used to test the value of `page_name` and adjust the `masthead_toy` image's link according to this value so that each section's page will display a different masthead toy image.

- A Multiple–Block–Parameters Hidden snippet is used as in #3, however unlike #3, it is used to set the value of another template parameter (`sectionimage`) which is then used to display the image.

- A template expression is used using an `if-then-else` construction to set each navigation button to the down state (and to remove its hyperlink) on the appropriate page; that is, on the FAQ page the FAQ button is unlinked and is set to the down state.

- An analogous method is used to set the `pageside_graphic` image to the correct value, just as was done for the `masthead_graphic` image.

- And, as a clean up, we changed the masthead graphic logic to use a method identical to that used for the `pageside_graphic`.

C h a p t e r 7

Building the Child Pages

Now that you've completed Chapter 6, "Building the Hot Cool Toys Base Template," you should have a template named HCTProject6.dwt available in your

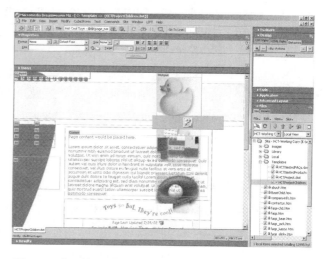

The completed base template.

site's `templates` folder. You will use this template exclusively for this section of the site construction. Don't worry if you didn't complete the navigation section because we are providing a completed template called `HCTProjectChildren.dwt` that you will use to complete this chapter. You also can examine a finished example we created using the instructions in this chapter by downloading the file `Finished_7.zip` from our support site at `www.dreamweavermx-templates.com/register.cfm`.

You have used template parameters, expressions, optional regions, `multipleIf` conditional regions, editable regions, and editable tag attributes to build what you have so far as a single Project template. You learned a lot in Chapter 6, and you will learn more in this chapter.

This chapter has several goals. We will be using the following template functions to create the child pages for the site from the master template you created in Chapter 6:

- Use Check Template Syntax
- Set parameters of the first generation pages
- Add page-specific content
- Add behaviors to the pages
- Use Detach from Template (optional)

Note

Note that none of these goals relate to the new template properties of DMX. If you are anxious to get to those items, you may want to skim this chapter quickly and move on to the next chapter.

There are many different ways to use each of these items in your own site and even in this site. We are presenting here what we consider to be the best method to use the described function within a project with this limited scope. We will not be exploring meta tags or search engine exposure at all in this chapter. If you are interested in learning about these items, please visit `www.spider-food.net`, which is an excellent resource for these subjects.

Warning

When you are using template parameters and expressions, the template can no longer be previewed in Internet Explorer (or Netscape Navigator, which doesn't even recognize the .dwt extension and wants to download the file!) because the specific template routines have not yet been run to produce the completed code for the page. To preview a template during this project without getting errors from IE, you *must* create a child page and preview the child page. (This is subject to your template being clean as a whistle, of course!)

Checking the Template Syntax

The very first thing that you must do is open the template file for the site (remember that you will be using either HCTProject6.dwt or HCTProjectChildren.dwt), and select Modify > Templates > Check Template Syntax.

If your template is built properly, you should get a confirmation dialog telling you Template Syntax is correct and displaying an OK button (see Figure 7.1). Click OK and close the template. If you get an error report, please go through Chapter 6 once again to figure out what is wrong with your template until you have achieved this confirmation dialog. The error report will tell you exactly which line number(s) contain which error(s) so that you can use that to figure out which section of Chapter 6 you need to go looking through to fix your issue. Alternatively, if your template (HCTProject6.dwt) has errors in it, you may opt to repair the issues later and proceed through this chapter using HCTProjectChildren.dwt as your source template.

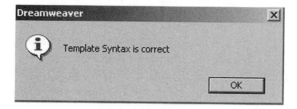

Figure 7.1   Template Syntax OK dialog.

Setting Desired Parameters

Let's get this chapter rolling by first creating all the required child pages of the template so that all the links will work. Then, you will modify the page_name parameter of each of these child pages to set the masthead, masthead_toy, sectionimage, and navigation button images.

Exercise 7.1:   Determining Page Names

The first thing you need to do is figure out what your page names are going to be. Fortunately, these values were already set for you in HCTProject.dwt, which means that if you performed the Chapter 6 exercises in their entirety, you should have a template named HCTProject6.dwt that has all expressions and links configured. If you chose not to do the exercises in Chapter 6, please use HCTProjectChildren.dwt as your starting template.

1. Select File > New > Templates Tab. In the Templates For: column, choose the site (HotCoolToys) and in the Site "HotCoolToys": column, choose HCTProjectChildren.dwt. Make sure that there is a check in the Update Page when Template Changes checkbox and click the Create button. See Figure 7.2 for the New from Template dialog.

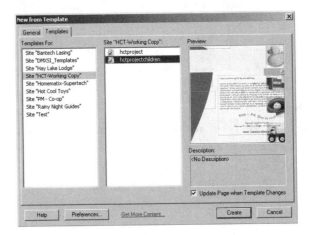

Figure 7.2   The New from Template dialog.

2. Select File > Save As, and in the Save As dialog, enter **index.htm** as the filename and click Save. (Index.htm/index.html are two of the default filenames configured by most hosts for the site—we will use the default filename of index.htm to make sure that it is the file that loads when the domain name only is used in the browser's address field.)

   Repeat this step five more times, using these filenames:

   • aboutus.htm
   • products.htm

- faqs.htm
- contactus.htm
- companyinfo.htm

You've just successfully created the entire web site for this project, but you're nowhere near finished. Read on.

The next thing that you need to do is open each of these child pages you just created and adjust the page_name parameter so that the appropriate navigation menu item (masthead, masthead_toy, or pageside_graphic) is displayed.

Note

For the purpose of this chapter, always make sure that the Allow Nested Templates To Control This checkbox is left empty.

3. So, with this task in mind, open index.htm, and select Modify > Template Properties. In the Template Properties dialog, select the page_name parameter and type in **Home** (which should already be the default value because of the way you built the template). Ensure that the Allow Nested Templates To Control This checkbox is empty and click the OK button. Select File > Save to save the changes to the page.

4. Repeat step 3 five more times, changing the value of page_name and the saved file name using Table 7.1 as a guide.

Table 7.1   HTML Filename/page_name Value Guide

Filename	Value for the page_name Parameter
index.htm	Home
aboutus.htm	About Us
products.htm	Our Products
faqs.htm	FAQs
contactus.htm	Contact Us
companyinfo.htm	Company Information

5. Close all open documents.

Congratulations! You've not only just built the entire site's pages, but you've also controlled the navigation menu states, the masthead image, the masthead_toy image, the pageside_graphic image, and the document's title, all by changing only one parameter: page_name.

Note

Note that you can change the values of `masthead` and `sectionimage` to your heart's content and the changes will have no effect on the pages. Those parameters are controlled by the value you set in `page_name`. We built that control in the template in the Chapter 6 exercise. This means that if you were the template designer and you passed the template to a content editor, you would advise the editor to change only the value of `page_name` in the child pages using the Modify > Template Properties menu item and Template Properties dialog. You should also pass on to the content editor what the allowed values are, but in case you forget, you already built the error message into the `MultipleIf` conditional region that displays these possible values in bright red text.

Well, now that the easy part is finished, you have to head into the harder part of this chapter: adding the content.

Adding Content

Inevitably, after creating the template, spawning the child pages, and setting the required parameters, you need to add content to your pages and upload them to the server. This section deals with setting content on the page in the editable region named Content (the only editable region in the template and second generation child pages). Now, let's get busy!

Note

This site is completely an invention of our mind's eye (and the graphic skill of Amy Santos)! Any resemblance to an existing company in part or whole is purely coincidental. Please do *not* send email to the email address in this demonstration, nor should you try to use any of the other contact information provided.

The Home Page

This page is the typical entry point for your visitor (new or returning) so it should be brief and to the point, providing a teaser to the site's content (in our case, an online Hot Cool Toy catalog of sorts).

Exercise 7.2:   Adding the Content to `index.htm`

Adding the content here is pretty straightforward. Here are the steps:

1. First, open `index.htm` in Dreamweaver MX.

2. Select the editable region content and replace it with the following text ({CR} means press Enter):

```
Welcome to our playground....
{CR}
Hot Cool Toys is the name of the site and the name of the content!
You'll find the latest and greatest toys here, usable by all ages
from newborn to the 100 year old kid in all of us.
{CR}
All toys have been extensively tested by our team at Hot Cool Toys,
and are guaranteed to last a lifetime. Now THAT is not something you
see every day, is it?
```

3. Select File > Save and your Home page is completed (see Figure 7.3).

4. Close the document and continue on to the next page.

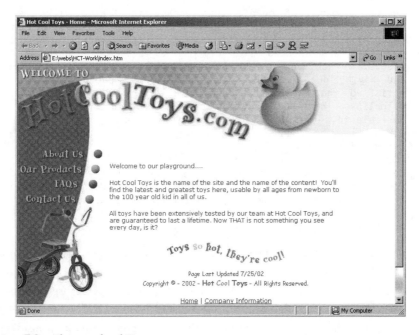

Figure 7.3   The completed Home page.

That's it—the content for the home page is finished!

The About Us Page

Content for this page should include such things as why the business is here (maybe a note from the company president would be appropriate), a mission statement, or a customer pledge.

Exercise 7.3:   Adding the Content to `aboutus.htm`

Adding the content here is also pretty straightforward, but on this page we add some heading tags.

1. The first thing you need to do is open `about.htm` in Dreamweaver MX.

2. Select the editable region content and replace it with the following text (`{CR}` means press Enter):

   We are a group of people that became frustrated with the lack of quality and the great expense of providing Hot Cool Toys to our children and each other through normal retail channels. We organized ourselves and created this company to circumvent both of these issues. We achieve this by dealing directly with the manufacturer and having our own test group work the products until we are satisfied that they will meet our high quality and durability guidelines. What this means to you is that you buy the best possible toys that will outlast your children.
   {CR}
   Our Mission Statement
   {CR}
   We promise to seek out the hottest, coolest toys to pass on to you at the best possible price by reducing overhead through the provision of these found products through online channels only.
   {CR}
   Our Pledge to You!
   {CR}
   We will provide the highest quality items at the best possible price, guaranteed!

3. Select the content `Our Mission Statement`, open the Property inspector (if it isn't already open), and in the drop-down field labeled `Format`, select Heading 2.

   Notice that the selected text turned purple and got larger to mark the heading for the section.

4. Repeat the process outlined in step number 3 with the content for Our Pledge to You.

5. Select File > Save, and your About Us page is completed (see Figure 7.4).

6. Close the document and continue on to the next page.

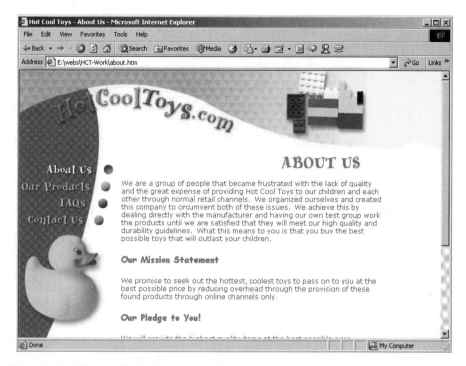

Figure 7.4   The completed About Us page.

Now the About Us page is finished.

The Contact Us Page

This page should contain detailed information for your mailing address, shipping address (if different from mailing address), telephone number (including country/area code), FAX number (including country/area code), and all pertinent email addresses for contact entry points in the organization.

Exercise 7.4:   Adding Content to `contactus.htm`

Adding the content here is also pretty simple, but on this page you add some heading tags and a table, and combine table columns.

1. First, open `contactus.htm` in Dreamweaver MX.

2. Select the editable region content and replace it with the following text:

   ```
   {CR}

   To provide you with the fastest possible service, please use one
   of the methods listed below if you need to contact us for any
   reason.
   ```

At this point, you have the basic textual content on the page, but you need to add a table in there, too.

3. For the purpose of this exercise, you are going to turn on accessibility features for tables. To do this, select Edit > Preferences. In the Preferences dialog, choose the Accessibility category and click Tables to select it. (For this exercise, all other accessibility features should be disabled). To save the change and close the dialog, click OK.

4. Position your cursor at the end of the text that reads contact us for any reason and press Enter. Select Insert > Table and in the dialog that pops up, enter the information listed in Table 7.2. Finally, click OK.

Table 7.2   Insert Background Table

Field	Entry
Rows:	1
Cell Padding:	0
Columns:	1
Cell Spacing:	0
Width:	100 Percent
Border:	0

After the dialog closes, a new dialog opens entitled Accessibility Options for Tables. For this table, simply click OK.

5. At this point, your single-celled table has been entered on the page and is currently selected. Open the Property inspector if necessary and change the Align field to Center. You'll notice that the change is immediate if you have split view enabled as per our instructions.

6. Position your cursor in the cell of this new table, and in the Bg: field in the Property inspector, enter **#FF9A00** and press the Tab key to activate the change. Your single-celled table now has an orange background color.

7. Leaving your cursor in the cell, insert another table, this time using the settings outlined in Table 7.3. Click OK when you're finished.

Table 7.3   Insert Inner Table

Field	Entry
Rows:	3
Cell Padding:	5
Columns:	2
Cell Spacing:	1
Width:	100 Percent
Border:	0

8. After you click OK, the Accessibility Features for Tables dialog reappears. Please complete the fields of the dialog as outlined in Table 7.4, clicking the OK button when you're finished to close the dialog.

Table 7.4   Inner Table Accessibility Features

Field Entry	
Caption:	Company Contact Information
Align Caption:	Top (Default places in the same position)
Summary:	Hot Cool Toys—Contact Information
Header:	Row

9. Select the top row of cells (beneath the caption text Company Contact Information) and using the Property inspector, type **#29D22D** in the Bg: field and press Tab to activate the change.

Note

You could use the color picker as well and disable Web Safe colors, but it would be difficult to pinpoint this exact html color, so it's best to type it instead. You may have to disable Web Safe colors in order to make the color stick. To do that, click the color picker, click the right arrow, and remove the checkmark beside Snap to Web Safe by clicking it.

The row should turn bright green. Now that all the coloring is done, it's time to enter content in this table.

10. Please fill in the table cells as shown in Table 7.5.

Table 7.5   Inner Table Content

Row	Column	Content
1	1	Mailing Address
1	2	Shipping Address
2	1	Hot Cool Toys {Shift+Enter}
		123 Some Street {Shift+Enter}
		This Town, That State {Shift+Enter}
		U.S.A. {Shift+Enter}
		98765
2	2	Hot Cool Toys {Shift+Enter}
		565 Another Street {Shift+Enter}
		This Town, That State {Shift+Enter}
		U.S.A. {Shift+Enter}
		98765

> **Note**
> You use {Shift+Enter} to force a line break <br> because you do not want blank lines between content lines. You also can control line spaces with CSS, but that is beyond the scope of this book.

11. Position your cursor in row 2, column 1 and using the Property inspector, change the value of the Width field to 50%. This forces the cells to be equal width for centering purposes.

12. Select the words Hot Cool Toys in row 2, column 1 and press Ctrl+B (Command+B) to change its properties to Bold (this might appear as Strong, depending on how your preferences are set).

13. Repeat step 12 for the same text in row 2, column 2.

14. Select row 3 and use Modify > Table > Merge Cells so that the two-column row will become a one-column-by-one-row cell.

15. Position your cursor in this cell and select Insert > Table. Please complete the dialog as shown in Table 7.6.

    You merged the cells and then inserted another table inside the merged cell because you don't want the orange border coloring to separate the items in this part of the content.

Table 7.6   Insert Nested Table Settings

Field	Entry
Rows:	3
Cell Padding:	5
Columns:	2
Cell Spacing:	1
Width:	100 Percent
Border:	0

Again, the Accessibility Options for Tables dialog appears. Simply click OK because you don't want any Accessibility features on this table. The table is added to the page in the cell where your cursor was positioned.

16. Using Table 7.7 as a guide, please fill in the data in the appropriate cells.

Table 7.7   Nested Table Content

Row	Column	Content
1	1	Telephone:
1	2	1.555.123.4567
2	1	Facsimile:
2	2	1.555.123.8901
3	1	E-mail:
3	2	info@hotcooltoys.com

17. Select the entire first row, and using the Property inspector, click the Bold icon in the upper right to boldface the contents of the cells. Then change the value of the Width field to 50%, and change the Alignment property Horz to Right.

18. Select the text info@hotcooltoys.com, and press Ctrl+C (Command+C) to copy this text to the clipboard. Open the Property inspector and in the Link field, type **mailto:** and press Ctrl+V (Command+V) to paste the clipboard contents into this field. The Link field should now look like this:

mailto:info@hotcooltoys.com

Press Tab to force the change in the Property inspector, and you've just made your first email link on the site.

19. Select File > Save to save the document. Figure 7.5 shows the completed page.

20. Close the document and continue on to the next page.

Figure 7.5   The completed Contact Us page.

Your Contact Us page is now completed.

The Company Information Page

You should include the company philosophy, investor information, and your stock designation or announcements for IPO (thinking big, of course) on this page.

Exercise 7.5:   Adding Content to `companyinfo.htm`

Once again, adding the content here also is simple.

1. Open `companyinfo.htm` in Dreamweaver MX.

2. Select the editable region content and replace it with the following text:

```
Investor Information
{CR}
Thinking of investing in our company? Please send your questions to
invest@hotcooltoys.com, providing your return mailing information.
Our staff will be delighted to ship you an investment information
package.
{CR}
Quarterly Report
{CR}
This report is not a de facto compilation, but rather a general
overview.
{CR}
Stock Market Information
{CR}
We are undertaking a public offering of stock in our company. The
IPO is slated for December 2002. Check back regularly for any
investor information updates on this page.
```

3. Select the content `Investor Information`, open the Property inspector, and in the Format drop-down field, select Heading 2. Notice that the selected text turned purple and got larger to mark the heading for the section.

4. Repeat the process in step 3 with the content `Quarterly Report` and `Stock Market Information`.

5. Select the text that reads `invest@hotcooltoys.com`, and press Ctrl+C (Command+C) to copy this text to the clipboard. Open the Property inspector and in the Link field, type **mailto:** and press Ctrl+V (Command+V) to paste the clipboard contents into this field. The Link field should now look like this:

   `mailto:invest@hotcooltoys.com`

   Press Tab to force the change in the Property inspector.

   Next, you need to add a table.

6. Position your cursor at the end of the text that reads `This report is not a de facto compilation, but rather a general overview` and press Enter. Select Insert > Table and in the dialog that pops up, enter the information listed earlier in Table 7.2 and click OK.

   When the Accessibility Options for Tables dialog appears, simply click the OK button. At this point, your single-celled table has been entered on the page and is currently selected.

7. Open the Property inspector and change the Align field to Center. Now, position your cursor in the cell of this new table and type **#FF9A00** in the Bg: field and press Tab to activate the change. Your single-celled table now has an orange background color.

8. Leaving your cursor in the cell, insert another table, this time using the settings outlined in Table 7.8. When you're done, click OK.

Table 7.8 Insert Inner Table

Field	Entry
Rows:	5
Cell Padding:	5
Columns:	4
Cell Spacing:	1
Width:	100 Percent
Border:	0

In the Accessibility Features for Tables dialog, please complete the fields of the dialog as outlined in Table 7.9. Click OK when you're done to close the dialog.

Table 7.9 Inner Table Accessibility Features

Field Entry	
Caption:	2001 Q-Statement—NET Align
Caption:	Top (Default places in the same position)
Summary:	2001 Quarterly Income/Expense/Profit Statement (NET)
Header:	Both

9. Select the top row of cells (beneath the caption text of 2001 Q-Statement—NET) and using the Property inspector, type **#29D22D** in the Bg: field ; then press Tab to activate the change. The row should turn a bright green color.

10. Now select the first column starting at row 2 and repeat step 9. You now have green on the top and left of the table!

11. Select the remaining orange cells starting at row 2 and column 2 and change the Bg: field of the Property inspector to **#FFFFFF**, pressing Tab to activate the change. The remaining cells change to a white background.

Now that all the coloring is done, it's time to enter content in this table.

12. Fill in the table cells as shown in Table 7.10.

Table 7.10   Inner Table Content

Row	Column	Content
1	1	Quarter
1	2	Income
1	3	Expense
1	4	Profit
2	1	1
2	2	$0
2	3	$0
2	4	$0
3	1	2
3	2	$100,201
3	3	$110,201
3	4	-$10,000
4	1	3
4	2	$254,000
4	3	$200,500
4	4	$53,500
5	1	4
5	2	$1,456,375
5	3	$456,375
5	4	$1,000,000

Whew, that was quite a bit to add to the table.

13. Select the content that reads -$10,000 and using the Tag Selector, click the <TD>.

In the Property inspector, beside the Format: drop down, you should see an icon. The icon is either a yellow A (showing HTML mode) or a silver oval with a fancy S in it (indicating CSS mode). This is the CSS/HTML Mode toggle. Clicking it changes the mode of operation back and forth between CSS and HTML. If the icon shows the yellow A, click it. When the icon shows the silver oval with the fancy S, select error from the drop-down immediately to the right of the icon. (This is known as the *CSS selector drop-down.*) The negative number should have turned red.

14. Select File > Save. The completed page is shown in Figure 7.6.

15. Close the document and continue on to the next page.

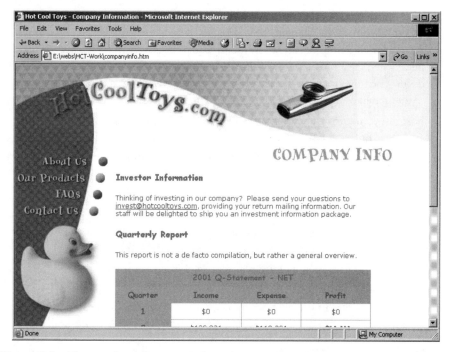

Figure 7.6   The completed Company Information page.

Your Company Information page is completed.

The Our Products Page

Now on to the meat of the site! This page should contain pictures of the product(s) with their names, a description (of each), part number/catalog number (of each), and the availability and price (U.S. dollars, of course). These items will be sorted alphabetically by product name in a table format.

Exercise 7.6:   Adding Content to `products.htm`

Adding the content here is pretty straightforward also.

1. Begin by opening `products.htm` in Dreamweaver MX.

2. Select the editable region content and replace it with the following text:

   ```
   To see the color image of the product, please position your
   mouse cursor over it. If you wish to go directly to the related FAQ
   section, please click the image.
   ```

Now you've got the basic text content on the page. If you read the text you are entering, you will realize that three things will be happening with these images. First, an image swap occurs when the mouse passes over, an image restore takes place when the mouse is moved off the image, and a link to an external page will occur when the image is clicked. (Each of these operations is explained in the "Adding Behaviors" section later in this chapter.)

3. Position your cursor at the end of the text that reads `please click the image` and press Enter.

4. Select Insert > Table and in the dialog that pops up, enter the information listed earlier in Table 7.2, and click OK.

   Click OK in the Accessibility Options for Tables dialog. At this point, your single-celled table has been entered on the page and is currently selected.

5. Open the Property inspector and change the Align field to `Center`.

6. Position your cursor in the cell of this new table and in the Bg: field of the Property inspector, type **#FF9A00** and press Tab to activate the change. Your single-celled table now has an orange background color.

7. Leave your cursor in the cell and insert another table, this time using the settings outlined in Table 7.11 and pressing the OK button when you're finished.

Table 7.11   Insert Inner Table

Field	Entry
Rows:	6
Cell Padding:	5
Columns:	4
Cell Spacing:	1
Width:	100 Percent
Border:	0

The Accessibility Features for Tables dialog opens. Please complete the fields of the dialog as shown in Table 7.12. Click OK when you're through to close the dialog.

Table 7.12   Inner Table Accessibility Features

Field	Entry
Caption:	Our Product List
Align Caption:	Top (Default places in the same position)
Summary:	2001 listing of our top 5 products
Header:	Both

8. Select the top row of cells (beneath the caption text of Our Product List) and in the Bg: field of the Property inspector, type **#29D22D** and press Tab. The row should turn a bright green color.

9. Now select the first column starting at row 2 and perform the same change in the Property inspector. You now have green on the top and left of the table.

10. Select the remaining orange cells starting at row 2 and column 2 and change the Bg: field of the Property inspector to **#FFFFFF**, pressing Tab to activate the change. The remaining cells change to a white background.

Next you need to enter content in this table.

11. Please fill in the table cells as you see in Table 7.13.

Table 7.13   Inner Table Content

Row	Column	Content
1	1	Item
1	2	Picture
1	3	Description
1	4	Price
2	1	1
2	2	{Leave Empty}
2	3	Teddy Bear
2	4	$32.99
3	1	2
3	2	{Leave Empty}
3	3	Jack in the Box
3	4	$21.99
4	1	3
4	2	{Leave Empty}
4	3	Krazy Kazoo
4	4	$5.99
5	1	4
5	2	{Leave Empty}
5	3	Slippery Slinky
5	4	$9.99
6	1	5
6	2	{Leave Empty}
6	3	Spinning Top
6	4	$18.99

That pretty much covers the main content of this page. The only thing left to do is add the images!

12. For the purpose of this page, you are going to turn on accessibility features for images. To do this, select Edit > Preferences. In the Preferences dialog, select the Accessibility category and click to select Images. (For this exercise, all other Accessibility features, excluding Tables, should be disabled.) To save the change and close the dialog, click OK button.

13. Position your cursor in row 2, column 2 (the cell should be empty and near the top of the table) and select Insert > Image to bring up the Select Image Source dialog.

    The Select File Name From: field should have the `HotCoolToys` folder in it. If it does not, navigate to this folder. Select the `images` folder, and then the `products` folder (this positions your image source at the correct folder for the product images).

    Select the image named `bear.jpg` and make sure that the Relative to: field is set to Document. Then click OK to insert the image and close the dialog. At this point, the Image Tag Accessibility Attributes dialog opens. Set the Alternate Text field to Teddy Bear and click the OK button to close the Accessibility dialog and complete the insertion of the image.

14. Using the previous instructions as outlined in step 13, please insert each image in the cell as shown in Table 7.14.

Table 7.14   Insert Product Images

Row	Column	Path to Image	Image	Alternate Text
3	2	`images/products/`	`jack.jpg`	Jack in the Box
4	2	`images/products/`	`kazoo.jpg`	Krazy Kazoo
5	2	`images/products/`	`slinky.jpg`	Slippery Slinky
6	2	`images/products/`	`top.jpg`	Spinning Top

15. Select File > Save. The completed page is shown in Figure 7.7.

16. Close the document and continue on to the next page.

Your Our Products page is completed.

The FAQs Page

As you would have on any site, this site needs frequently asked questions. These questions will be directly related to the company's products and be sorted by product name in a table format. Each product will have its own table—you'll see why in a minute.

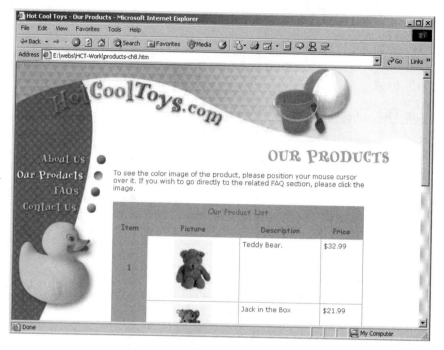

Figure 7.7   The completed Our Products page.

Exercise 7.7:   Adding Content to the FAQs Page

Again, adding the content here is pretty straightforward.

1. First, open `faqs.htm` in Dreamweaver MX.

2. Select the editable region content and delete it. With your cursor still positioned inside the editable region named `Content`, press Enter several times (8 to be safe). You do this to make sure that you have enough space to use as table separators for the tables because it is a bit more challenging to separate inserted tables after the fact.

3. Using Code view, locate the very first `<p> </p>` tag pair in the editable region named `Content`, and type the following:

    Quick Links » Bear | Jack | Kazoo | Slinky | Top

 Note

» is a character entity. If you want to use Design view to enter this character, open the Insert bar, click the Characters tab, and click the Other Characters button on the far right end of the bar.

4. Using Design view, position your cursor at the end of the preceding line and press Enter. (Alternatively, you can position the cursor in the next empty line that you added at the beginning of this exercise.) Insert a table using Insert > Table and use the values listed in Table 7.15 to complete the Insert Table dialog. Click OK.

Table 7.15   Insert the First Table

Field	Entry
Rows:	4
Cell Padding:	5
Columns:	2
Cell Spacing:	1
Width:	100 Percent
Border:	0

After you've clicked OK, the Accessibility Features for Tables dialog opens.

5. Please complete the fields of the dialog as outlined in Table 7.16, clicking OK when you're finished to close the dialog.

Table 7.16   First Table Accessibility Features

Field	Entry
Caption:	Teddy Bear FAQ
Align Caption:	Top (Default places in the same position)
Summary:	FAQ concerning the Teddy Bear
Header:	None

6. Fill in this table with the content specified in Table 7.17

Table 7.17   First Table Content

Row	Column	Content
1	1	Q
1	2	Enter your own question here
2	1	A
2	2	Enter your own answer here
3	1	Q
3	2	Enter your own question here
4	1	A
4	2	Enter your own answer here

7. In the line immediately below this table, type the following:

Top of Page{CR}

8. Repeat steps 4 through 7 four more times, using the information given in Table 7.18.

Table 7.18   Accessibility Content

Table	Caption	Align Caption	Summary	Header
2	Jack in the Box FAQ	Top	FAQ concerning the Jack in the Box	None
3	Krazy Kazoo FAQ	Top	FAQ concerning the Krazy Kazoo	None
4	Slippery Slink FAQ	Top	FAQ concerning the Slippery Slinky	None
5	Spinning Top FAQ	Top	FAQ concerning the Spinning Top	None

9. For each `Top of Page` text entry, select it and using the Property inspector, change the Link: field to `javascript:window.scrollTo(0,0);` and press Tab to activate the change.

We use this method to circumvent a Netscape 4.x issue that causes "empty" named anchors in layers and tables not to function properly. So, this step should be performed five times, once for each `Top of Page` entry.

10. You see the five captions displayed on the page, one for each table. Starting at the top (Teddy Bear FAQ), insert a named anchor at the beginning of the caption, using Insert > Named Anchor. Complete the Named Anchor dialog using `tbear` and click OK.

11. Repeat step 10 for each of the captions, defining the Named Anchor as outlined in Table 7.19. The completed document is shown in Figure 7.8.

Note

You used unique tables for each FAQ section because Netscape 4.x has an issue in which it doesn't exactly position itself very well to named anchors when the named anchor link is clicked inside layers and large tables. To circumvent this, this example uses a unique table for each FAQ section and a named anchor for each, which Netscape 4.x will accept. There is still one outstanding issue for which there is no known workaround: Netscape 4.x will not scroll to anchored text when the text is in a layer from an external page link, as you will see in the section "Adding Behaviors" coming up.

Table 7.19   Accessibility Content

Table	Caption	Named Anchor
2	Jack in the Box FAQ	`jib`
3	Krazy Kazoo FAQ	`kkaz`
4	Slippery Slink FAQ	`slink_`
5	Spinning Top FAQ	`stop`

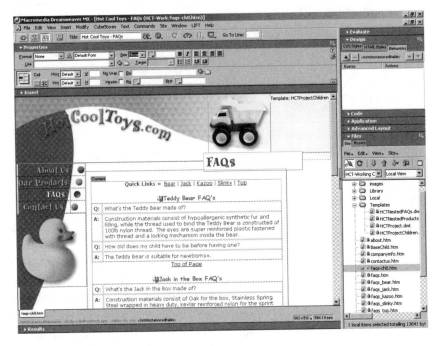

Figure 7.8   Completed document with anchors added.

12. Remember the entered text at the very top that indicated Quick Links? Scroll to this content in Design view and select the word Bear. Using the Property inspector, change the Link: field to #tbear and press Tab to activate the change.

13. Repeat step 12 for each item in this row using the information in Table 7.20 as a guide.

Table 7.20   Named Anchor Link Information

Link Word	Link Field of Property Inspector
Jack	`#jib`
Kazoo	`#kkaz`
Slinky	`#slink`
Top	`#stop`

14. Select the text Quick Links >> at the top of the page and press Ctrl+B (Command+B) to boldface it.

15. Select each table's first column independently (this should be the column containing the Qs and As) and press Ctrl+B (Command+B) to apply bold. Repeat for the first column of each table.

16. If there are any extra paragraphs beneath the Top of Page link of the bottom table, delete them by positioning your cursor in the last one and pressing the backspace key until you get to the Top of Page link.

17. Save the page using File > Save.

18. Close any open documents.

There was quite a bit to do to this page: You added links (a submenu system of sorts), named anchors so that you could get to the appropriate FAQ section quickly, and added Top of Page links to get to the menu/submenu quickly and easily.

Adding Behaviors

You will want to add behaviors to your child pages eventually, and this section shows you how to add a behavior that provides an image roll effect to the product images of the products page.

Exercise 7.8:   Add a Behavior to the Products Page

To add a behavior, do the following:

1. First, open products.htm in Dreamweaver MX.

   Prepare the images first before adding any behaviors. As you will recall, you want the image to swap when the mouse pointer is over the image, swap back when the pointer is off the image, and when the image is clicked, you want the image to act as a link to the FAQ section. The first thing you need to do is go through the five images and give them a name as well as a link.

2. Select the Teddy Bear image, and in the Property inspector, change the Name field to **img_item_1** and change the Link: field to **faqs.htm#tbear**. (You're linking directly to your named anchor on the FAQs page. Note that Netscape 4.x will not automatically scroll to the targeted named anchor of the **faqs.htm** page.) Press Tab to activate the changes.

 Note

Each image must have a unique name in order for the image swap to occur without issue.

3. Repeat step 3 for each image, as you see in Table 7.21.

Table 7.21   Image Settings

Image	PI Name	PI Link
Jack in the Box	`img_item_2`	`faqs.htm#jib`
Krazy Kazoo	`img_item_3`	`faqs.htm#kkaz`
Slippery Slinky	`img_item_4`	`faqs.htm#slink`
Spinning Top	`img_item_5`	`faqs.htm#stop`

4. Select the `Teddy Bear` image and open your Behaviors panel (Window > Behaviors). In the Behaviors panel, click the plus (+) button to activate the menu, scroll down to Show Events For and make sure there is a check beside 4.0 and Later Browsers. If there is not, select this menu item and the check will appear, indicating that it is selected.

5. Click the plus (+) button again, and then locate and choose Swap Image. The Swap Image dialog opens with the selected image highlighted. In the Set Source To field, navigate to the image named `bear_c.jpg` in the `images/products` folder. Ensure that there is a check in Preload Images and Restore Images onMouseOut, and then click OK.

Several things happen at this point. The image line changes from this:

```
<a href="faqs.htm#tbear"><img src="images/products/bear.jpg"
alt="Teddy Bear" name="img_item_1" width="72" height="108"
border="0" id="img_item_1"></a>
```

to this:

```
<a href="faqs.htm#tbear"
onMouseOver="MM_swapImage('img_item_1','','images/products/bear_c.j
pg',1)" onMouseOut="MM_swapImgRestore()"><img src="images/prod-
ucts/bear.jpg" alt="Teddy Bear" name="img_item_1" width="72"
height="108" border="0" id="img_item_1"></a>
```

The over image is added to the body tag `onLoad` event (even though it is in a locked region), and no JavaScript code is added to the page (because the image swap JavaScript code is used in the template itself so no modification is required).

Note

Be aware that you should select each image individually and then apply the Swap Image behavior. It is a common mistake for people new to the software to inadvertently keep applying the different Swap Image behaviors to the same image, thereby causing all images to swap when the first image is moused over and none of the others work as expected when moused over. This can be one of those *gotchas* that is similar to the image naming issue!

Warning

A bug exists that overwrites the child page body events when the child page is updated by the template. Because this page adds images to the preload behavior of the `onLoad` event, subsequent updates will force you to re-inspect the behaviors to reapply this page's additional image preloads. For details, see the technote at `www.macromedia.com/go/16366`.

6. Repeat step 5 for each image in the list, using the information in Table 7.22 as a guide.

Table 7.22   Image Swap Data

Image	Path to Roll	Roll Image
Jack in the Box	`images/products`	`jack_c.jpg`
Krazy Kazoo	`images/products`	`kazoo.jpg`
Slippery Slinky	`images/products`	`slinky_c.jpg`
Spinning Top	`images/products`	`top_c.jpg`

7. Select File > Save.

8. Close the document.

Your Our Products page is completed.

Detaching the Site from the Template

The template markup isn't so heavy in this site, which consists of six pages, but you may decide that you want to remove the markup to decrease load times just that much more.

Exercise 7.9:   Removing Template Markup

We covered the various ways of removing Dreamweaver markup in Chapter 4, "Removing Dreamweaver Markup." You will be using the Export Site Without Markup method in this exercise because you are doing an entire site and want no markup left on the page to minimize page load times.

1. Open `index.htm`. (You actually can use any of the site files, but we like to start with the site's default start page for simplicity's sake.)

2. Select Modify > Templates > Export Without Markup.

The Export Site Without Template Markup dialog opens, where you should remove the check in Keep Template Data Files and Extract Only Changed Files.

Click the Browse button to navigate to your export folder.

Warning

Do not export your site into any folder, existing or new, that is within your existing site structure. Use a completely new and unique location! Here's why you don't want to do that:

- You could overwrite your template-based child pages with detached pages.
- Dreamweaver can get confused when exporting the site in this manner and toast the site.

Navigate to your local drive, and using the New Folder icon, create a new folder and name it **Exported_Site**. Double-click this new folder and click the Select button in the Extract Template XML dialog. Click OK on the Export Site Without Template Markup dialog and Dreamweaver does its magic. Create a new site folder structure in the defined folder, copy all required files from the site, and remove any and all Dreamweaver Template Markup while leaving library item information intact.

3. Using your file manager, navigate to this new folder and preview the site in your browser. Everything should work exactly as it did with Template Markup intact; however, template changes will not be propagated to this site location because the child pages are no longer associated with the template and the folder is outside of the scope of the original defined site.

4. Hmm…this poses a problem. How do you upload the site to the server? Well, you simply need to create a new site definition in Dreamweaver for this new site location, and you will be good to go!

5. Close all open documents.

That's all there is to exporting a site while stripping the template markup out of it at the same time.

Did you notice that the exported site has the Templates and Library folder intact in the new site's folder structure? Editing the .lbi files will update the pages but editing the .dwt files won't. Keep that in mind when you go to do some editing of your templates in this site definition.

Summary

You've done many things with the template in this chapter. You have checked your template syntax to make sure that it is OK, created your child pages, set the child page parameters, modified each child page to add content, added behaviors to cause an image swap, created named anchors and links to those named anchors, and exported the site so that template markup was stripped out of the code.

This chapter doesn't teach you anything new, however; it does teach you in a real-world environment how to actually perform the items described in Section I of the book.

Chapter 8

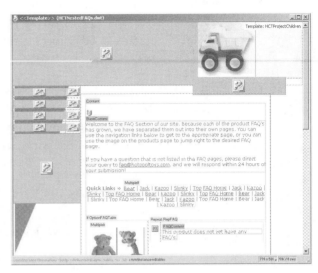

The nested FAQ template.

Modifications to the Site

As with most options in DMX, there are different ways to make the templates and pages in the site—sometimes the biggest challenge we face is choosing between these options! The first choice in this chapter concerns what to do when you want more than one product page or you want to place each FAQ section in its own page. Although the task may sound complex, deciding how to do it within the parent template's control is logically sensible and pretty easy to do, as you will see in this chapter. Furthermore, this logic is portable to other pages in this or other sites! Please feel free to modify the process as you see fit once you learn how.

Building on what you learned in Chapters 6 and 7, you will now enhance the site by placing each FAQ section in the FAQ page group on its own page, keeping the pages easily editable for the content editor. You can accomplish both of these tasks by creating and using nested templates. For clarity, let's separate these two tasks as follows:

- Enhancing the Products page
- Creating multiple FAQ pages

But first...read and heed "Nested Template Issues and Work-Arounds"!

Nested Template Issues and Work-Arounds

Before you begin working with pages, you need to know about a few nested template issues. We trust their importance will become obvious as you read them.

When you create a nested template, images referenced by expressions in the parent template display until you save the nested template. After the nested template is saved, the images become broken image links. The reason for this is that the nested template is based on the evaluation of the parent template expressions, thereby rendering the broken links (in the nested template only). Any child pages of these nested templates will display the images just fine, subject to the proper location of the second-generation child pages in the folder structure.

The MUI (mini-user interface) that is used to control the addition, removal, and repositioning of repeating regions and repeating tables no longer functions. This is a confirmed bug in DMX only that occurs when the repeating table is in a positioned layer (as in this example) or there is CSS-P applied to the repeating table's table tag. Luckily, there is a simple work-around: Position the cursor in a repeating region, right-click (Control+click) to display the context menu, and select the Templates. If you prefer, you can choose Modify > Templates > Repeating Entries menu system to perform these tasks, instead of using the MUI.

> **Note**
>
> If you don't want to choose the menu items for this feature, you can assign keyboard shortcuts to select Modify > Templates > as an interim solution. (For detailed instructions, see Chapter 34, "Customizing Dreamweaver," in *Inside Dreamweaver MX* by Laura Gutman et al. (New Riders Publishing).

When you save a nested template after modifying it, its state does not change to saved. The file still displays the * marker, showing it as modified. This is a confirmed bug in DMX, and the reason for it is that the template engine is updating the nested template as well as its child pages. There is a work-around, although it can be a little bit of a nuisance to use. The solution is to not save any changes to the nested template until you close it.

This is not to say, "Don't save your work often" as that simply is not the case; you should save the template as often as you want. Just be advised to NOT update pages until you are finished with the template for the day, then on closing the template, save the last bit of changes and update the site.

So, the procedure is to use File > Close, and when prompted to save changes, select Yes. When prompted to update child pages of the nested template, choose Update and the proper files will be updated. To make further changes to the nested template, reopen it for editing and repeat as needed.

Last, there is a bug in the template engine that can possibly corrupt your nested template or child page `body onLoad` event. For more information, read *Technote 16366* (`www.macromedia.com/go/16366`). As an addendum to this tech note, we found that if your child page uses additional swap image behaviors with preloading of images set to On, any subsequent updates from the template or nested template will overwrite the same `body onLoad` event. A work-around is to open the child page and re-inspect each swap image behavior that is in an editable region, save the page, and upload it to the server. It doesn't really affect the functionality of the document, but it may be a small nuisance if you're counting on those preloaded images.

Setting Up the Nested Templates

Chapter 3, "All About Templates and Regions," covered the basics of nested templates, and you will apply and build on that knowledge in the following exercise group.

Exercise 8.1:   Creating the Base Nested Templates

The first thing you need to do is prep your already-created pages and create your nested templates. You'll use the same process for both the Products page and the FAQs page.

1. Using the site panel/window, rename products.htm to products-ch7.htm (when prompted to update links, select No). Repeat this for faqs.htm by renaming it to faqs-ch7.htm and electing not to update links.

   You don't want to update the links because you don't want all your other references on the other pages of the site to get changed. You will continue using products.htm and faqs.htm with your nested templates so the links must stay as they are. We've simply created backups of our work from the previous chapter.

Note

Resist your first inclination to open products.htm and faqs.htm and save them as templates. Although this will work, it will not give you a great reference point from which to build the required nested templates for each page or page group. With this in mind, you will be creating your nested templates from scratch.

2. Select File > New to open the New Document dialog. Click the Templates tab and select your site (HotCoolToys) from the Templates for: column. In the Site column, select the template named HCTProjectChildren. Ensure that there is a check in the Update Page when Template Changes box and click Create.

3. Immediately save this file as BaseChild.htm. This file will not be referenced in page links or anything else; it is created strictly to generate the required nested templates for the site.

4. With the file still open, select File > Save as Template, type **HCTNestedFAQs**, and click Save. Now, choose File > Save As, resave the nested template as **HCTNestedProducts.dwt**, and close all open documents.

That's all there is to the creation of the nested templates. To recap, create your initial template, create a child page of that template, and then save the child as a template.

You've just successfully saved an archival copy of your faqs.htm and products.htm pages from Chapter 7 and created the two required nested templates you will be building next.

Enhancing the Products Page

The Products page lends itself to nesting because you may want only a certain number of products on each page, but you initially might have only enough products to create a single Products sub-page. This section of the chapter teaches you the basics of nesting templates and shows you how to create child pages from that nested template. You can easily apply what you will learn in Exercise 8.2 to this nested template.

Exercise 8.2:   Building the Products Nested Template

Let's set our goals for this nested template first. Our main objective is to create a nested template with the table already built on it. This ensures that the content editor can easily add and remove products from the table without having to know HTML or having to use multiple menu items to create and remove additional content.

Note

A *content editor* is a person who has nothing to do with the construction of the site templates, but who does use the templates to create child pages for the site and edit the content of those child pages.

1. Open the template named HCTNestedProducts and select Modify > Template Properties. Choose the page_name parameter and change the value from Home to Our Products, clicking OK to close the Template Properties dialog and set the images and navigation for the nested template.

2. Select the entire editable region contents and type the following ({CR} means press Enter): To see the color image of the product, please position your mouse cursor over it. If you wish to go directly to the related FAQ section, please click the image.{CR}

   You don't want the content editor to be able to change the contents of the entire editable region, so in order to prevent that, add a new editable region inside the Content editable region. Position your cursor at the end of the line containing the text please click the image and press Enter to force a new paragraph.

3. Select the Insert > Table menu item and in the dialog that pops up, enter the information listed in Table 8.1 and click OK.

Table 8.1   Insert Background Table

Field	Entry
Rows:	2
Cell Padding:	0
Columns:	1
Cell Spacing:	0
Width:	100 percent
Border:	0

4. The Accessibility Options for Tables dialog opens. For this table, simply click OK.

5. At this point, your single-celled table has been entered on the page and is currently selected. Open the Property inspector if necessary and change the Align field to Center and in the Bg: field, type **#FF9A00**. Press Tab to activate the change.

   Your single-celled table now has a background color of Orange and is centered.

6. Position your cursor in the orange cell and insert another table, this time using the properties outlined in Table 8.2 for the Insert Table dialog and the Accessibility dialog properties.

Table 8.2   Inner Table Properties

Field	Entry
Rows:	2
Cell Padding:	5
Columns:	4
Cell Spacing:	1
Width:	100 percent
Border:	0
Caption:	2001 listing of our top 5 products
Align Caption:	Top
Summary:	Our Product List
Header:	Both

7. Select the entire top row (four columns) and change the Property inspector's Bg: field to **#29D22D**. Press Tab key to activate the change.

8. Type the following words in the cells (from left to right): **Item, Picture, Description, Price.**

9. Select the leftmost cell of the second row and change the Property inspector's Bg: field to **#29D22D**. Press Tab.

10. Select the remaining cells that are not colored green, change the Bg: field to **#FFFFFF**, and press Tab.

11. Select the entire bottom row (four cells) and choose Insert > Template Objects > Repeating Region. In the dialog that pops up, give the repeating region the name of **RepProducts** and click OK to complete the insertion.

12. Position your cursor in the leftmost cell of the repeating region, switch to Code view, and type @@(_index+1)@@ (if there is an , delete it).

What's this doing? you ask. Why, it takes the row number (dynamically calculated by the template engine starting at this repeating region) and displays it in this cell. We add a 1 to it because we want the numbering to start at 1, not 0. Switch back to Design view and select the second cell of the repeating row.

13. Select Insert > Template Objects > Editable Region. In the dialog that appears, type **Picture** and click the OK button.

14. Repeat step 13 for the two remaining cells of this row, substituting **Description** and **Price** for the editable region names when prompted by the dialog.

But, this is a repeating table! you say. Well, yes and no. We can do almost exactly the same thing by inserting a repeating table; however, the repeating table dialog does not bring the accessibility dialog to life, which means that we lose that functionality; also, using the repeating table makes each cell of a row an editable region, and you would have to manually change the editable region names from their default insertion names. Yes, you can manually remove the first editable region and change the region names and add the accessibility features, but either way, you are not saving any time or keystrokes. The way we relate here does display the Accessibility dialog and allows us to name our editable regions properly, which is what we really want.

There are only a couple of things left to change on this template before you can make your new `products.htm` page, so let's continue with the exercise.

15. Position your cursor in the editable region named `Picture` and in the Property inspector, change the Horz: value to `Center` and Vert: value to `Top`.

16. Reposition your cursor in the `Description` editable region and change the value of Vert: in the Property inspector to `Top`.

17. Reposition your cursor yet again in the editable region named `Price` and using the Property inspector, change the value of the Vert: field to `Top`.

The last thing we are going to do in this template is pre-format the cells for display in USD (U.S. dollars) by adding a bold dollar sign ($).

18. Position your cursor in the second row, fourth column immediately prior to the editable region named `Price` and type **$**. Using your mouse, select the entire contents of this cell (so that the cell is highlighted) and press Ctrl+B (Command+B) to bold it.

Note

If you do not select the entire cell, DMX will bold the contents incorrectly and write another editable region to the page, thereby causing you problems down the road due to duplicate region names. If you're having difficulty selecting the cell or its contents, position your cursor in the desired cell, use the Tag Selector to select the <TD>, and then press Ctrl+B (Command+B) to make the cell contents bold (strong). Besides, we only really want one editable region in this cell!

You also might want to change the default editable region text from `Price` to `00.00` so that there is a visual clue that a value needs to be entered. You do that by selecting the contents of the editable region named `Price` and typing **00.00**, which should replace the previous contents of the editable region.

19. Close the template, and when prompted, *make sure* that you save the changes and update pages if asked.

Reopen this template (`HCTNestedProducts.dwt`) and notice two things. First and most important, the images are all image placeholders now. This happens due to the method we used to call the images (discussed in Chapter 6, "Building the Hot Cool Toys Base Template"). Notice also that the original editable region named Content is now highlighted as orange. This means that the contents of this cell are locked because there are nested editable regions inside it—and anything you type outside of the new editable regions will not be changeable in the child page of this template. Close the template document (you should not be prompted to save or update at this point).

Whew—that was pretty easy, actually, but it had quite a few steps.

20. There's only one more thing you need to know about this template, so let's continue by selecting File > New, clicking the Templates tab, and choosing the newly created nested template named HCTNestedProducts.dwt. Make sure there is a check in the Update Page When Template Changes field and click Create.

21. Immediately save this new file as products.htm in the site root by using File > Save As.

22. Add your base image (the link and the behaviors as described in Chapter 7) in the editable region named Picture, the content of the description in the editable region named Description, and the price of this product in the editable region named Price. Now try to use the MUI to add another row—it doesn't work!

If you go back to the section "Nested Template Issues and Work-Arounds" and take a look at the second bulleted item, you will see the reasons for this. Don't worry, though—you can use two menu items to add and reposition the rows of the repeating table. The first is Modify > Templates > Repeating Entries. You also can use the context menu by right-clicking (Ctrl+click)and selecting Templates.

The finished template is shown in Figure 8.1.

 Note

Because the context menu is easier to navigate and contains more commands for repeating tables, we tend to use this method more than the other method.

Adding content is discussed in Chapter 7, so feel free to refer to those instructions and add any content you need for your products. We recommend holding off on adding the links to the images other than using javascript:; because we haven't covered the FAQ nested template and pages yet. That's next on the agenda!

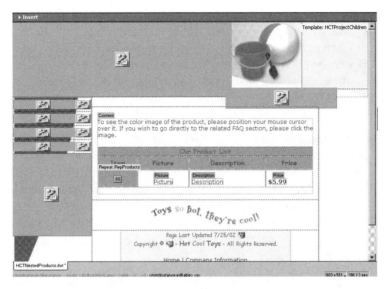

Figure 8.1   The finished nested products template.

Creating Multiple FAQ Pages

The FAQ pages is an excellent example for making a multipurpose nested template because you may want each Products FAQ to have its own page, and you also need a base FAQ page acting as a FAQ Home for the base site's menu system. This section of the chapter teaches you about the more advanced techniques of nesting templates and the creation of child pages from that nested template.

Exercise 8.3:   Building the FAQ Nested Template

Similar to the process in the previous section, you first need to set your goals for the nested template. Your main objective is to create a nested template that can be used as the FAQ area default page and also be used for each individual FAQ page. With this in mind, you need to have a content area for the base FAQ page, a sub-navigational system so that you can get to each FAQ sub-page, as well as a repeating table for the FAQ pages themselves. The sub-navigation needs to be available on all pages, the content area of the FAQ base shows only on this page, and the repeating table shows only on the FAQ sub-pages. The last thing you want is all of this controlled through one nested template.

You need to think about page names next. The default FAQ home page is going to be named `faqs.htm` so that your other template links aren't affected (this is why you renamed `faqs.htm` to `faqs-ch7.htm` in the setup for this chapter). Next, you want each FAQ sub-page to be easily identifiable. Thus, you will add `faqs_` to each FAQ sub-page name and use the product name as the remainder of the page name. This means that pages will be named `faqs_bear.htm`, `faqs_jack.htm`, `faqs_kazoo.htm`, `faqs_slinky.htm`, and `faqs_top.htm`.

1. Open `products.htm` and make sure that you select each image in the product list and link it to the desired FAQ page. The pages don't exist yet, so you will have to type the link for each image using the Property inspector Link: field. There should be no folder navigation because all files are in the site root—the links will simply be `faqs_blah.htm` as outlined in the preceding paragraph). Press Tab to make the change, and repeat for the remaining images. When the process is completed, save and close `products.htm`. You won't be needing it again for the remainder of this chapter.

2. Open the file `HCTNestedFAQs.dwt` and let's get started creating our complex template. Select all the content in the editable region named Content and delete it. We will not be using any of it for this template. Press Enter a couple of times to make sure that there is enough blank space on the page to work with.

3. Position your cursor on the first line of the editable region named Content and insert an editable optional region using Insert > Template Objects > Editable Optional Region.

   You know from Chapter 4 that this inserts a Boolean parameter in the head, an optional region in the body, and an editable region inside the optional region. Unfortunately, the Insert Optional Region dialog does not provide you with a method of renaming the editable region, so it is added to the page as `EditRegion2` (the name of your region may differ slightly). Rename this to `BaseContent`.

4. Position your cursor in the editable region and the Property inspector should change to the Editable Region Property inspector with the Name: field being populated by `EditRegion2` (if the Property inspector doesn't display using this method, please use the Tag Selector and select the nearest tag entitled `<mmtemplate:editable>` which will always change the Property inspector to the proper configuration). Change the value to `BaseContent` and press the Tab key to effect the change.

5. Position your cursor in the editable region named `BaseContent` and type the following:

```
Welcome to the FAQ Section of our site. Because each of the
product FAQs has grown, we have separated them out into their
own pages. You can use the navigation links below to get to the
appropriate page, or you can use the image on the products page
to jump right to the desired FAQ page.{CR}
```

> If you have a question that is not listed in the FAQ pages, please direct your query to faq@hotcooltoys.com, and we will respond within 24 hours of your submission!

6. Select the text that reads:

```
faq@hotcooltoys.com
```

Press Ctrl+C (Command+C) to copy it to the clipboard. Type **mailto:** in the Property inspector's Link: field and press Ctrl+V (Command+V) to paste the clipboard contents. The link should appear as follows:

```
mailto:faq@hotcooltoys.com
```

Press the Tab key to make the changes.

Next, you will work on the FAQ sub-links. You position this after the preceding content because you always want the sub-links below the FAQ introductory text.

7. Position your cursor on the next available blank line below the optional region named `BaseContent`. Switch to Code view and type the following:

**Quick Links » **

Switch back to Design view and select the text `Quick Links >>`. Using the property inspector, click the B icon and the Center icon, which boldfaces and centers the sub-navigation system in the layer table.

Next, you need to add the links. Although you can easily add each link to the menu system and force them all to be live at one time, we want to go one step further and hide the link that represents the currently displayed page. There are a couple of ways you can do this:

- You can set up optional regions for each link and use template properties to display or hide each as required on the child pages.

- You can use a `multipleif` conditional statement and have each link system in its own separate `if` and base the expression result on a new parameter. You'll use this method later in this chapter.

8. Using Code view, position your cursor in the editable region named `Head` (make sure you're not in the middle of any other content in this region), and using the Snippets panel, insert the snippet labeled `Text` located in the Templates > Parameters folder. Edit the parameter by hand to ensure that your parameter statement looks like this:

```
<!-- TemplateParam name="faqName" type="text" value="home" -->
```

What you're doing here is setting up the parameter used to evaluate the `multipleif` conditional statements. The content editor of the site will be able to change the parameter by accessing Modify > Template Properties from the child page.

9. Switch back to Design view and place your cursor at the end of the line containing `Quick Links >>`. Using the Snippets panel again, insert the snippet entitled `M_Block Text` located in the `Templates > If` folder.

10. Modify the inserted code using Code view to look like the following code fragment:

Note

This following fragment is quite a bit to type, so we have provided the code as a text file you can copy and paste into Code view of the template. The code fragment is named `codefrag1.txt` and available in the folder named `Local`).

```
<!-- TemplateBeginMultipleIf -->
      <!-- TemplateBeginIfClause cond="faqName=='home'" -->
<a href="../faqs_bear.htm">Bear</a> | <a
href="../faqs_jack.htm">Jack</a> | <a
href="../faqs_kazoo.htm">Kazoo</a> | <a
href="../faqs_slinky.htm">Slinky</a> | <a
href="../faqs_top.htm">Top</a><!-- TemplateEndIfClause -->
      <!-- TemplateBeginIfClause cond="faqName=='bear'" -->
<a href="../faqs.htm">FAQ Home</a> | <a
href="../faqs_jack.htm">Jack</a> | <a
href="../faqs_kazoo.htm">Kazoo</a> | <a
href="../faqs_slinky.htm">Slinky</a> | <a
href="../faqs_top.htm">Top</a><!-- TemplateEndIfClause -->
      <!-- TemplateBeginIfClause cond="faqName=='jack'" -->
<a href="../faqs.htm">FAQ Home</a> | <a
href="../faqs_bear.htm">Bear</a> | <a
href="../faqs_kazoo.htm">Kazoo</a> | <a
href="../faqs_slinky.htm">Slinky</a> | <a
href="../faqs_top.htm">Top</a><!-- TemplateEndIfClause -->
      <!-- TemplateBeginIfClause cond="faqName=='kazoo'" -->
<a href="../faqs.htm">FAQ Home</a> | <a
href="../faqs_bear.htm">Bear</a> | <a
href="../faqs_jack.htm">Jack</a> | <a
href="../faqs_slinky.htm">Slinky</a> | <a
href="../faqs_top.htm">Top</a><!-- TemplateEndIfClause -->
      <!-- TemplateBeginIfClause cond="faqName=='slinky'" -->
<a href="../faqs.htm">FAQ Home</a> | <a
href="../faqs_bear.htm">Bear</a> | <a
href="../faqs_jack.htm">Jack</a> | <a
href="../faqs_kazoo.htm">Kazoo</a> | <a
href="../faqs_top.htm">Top</a><!— TemplateEndIfClause -->
      <!-- TemplateBeginIfClause cond="faqName=='top'" -->
<a href="../faqs.htm">FAQ Home</a> | <a
href="../faqs_bear.htm">Bear</a> | <a
href="../faqs_jack.htm">Jack</a> | <a
href="../faqs_kazoo.htm">Kazoo</a> | <a
href="../faqs_slinky.htm">Slinky</a><!-- TemplateEndIfClause -->
<!-- TemplateEndMultipleIf -->
```

Here you've set a specific set of links to display depending on the value of `faqName`, which is editable by the content editor. In other words, if you are on the "jack in the box" page, why would you want the link to the same page to be present and functional?

11. Using Design view, position your cursor at the next available blank line below this `multipleif` conditional region. Insert an optional region using Insert > Template Objects > Optional Region. Use the name `OptionFAQTable` in the Optional Region dialog and click the dialog's OK button to set the change, insert the optional region, and close the dialog.

12. Position your cursor inside the new optional region and insert a table with the specifications shown in Table 8.3.

Table 8.3   Optional Region Table Settings

Field	Entry
Rows:	2
Cell Padding:	5
Columns:	2
Cell Spacing:	0
Width:	100 Percent
Border:	0

The Accessibility Options for Tables dialog appears. Click OK. At this point, your table has been entered on the page and is currently selected.

13. Position your cursor in the top left cell, and using the Property inspector, change the value of Vert: to `Top` and Horz: to `Center`. Repeat for the top right cell and the bottom left cell. For the bottom right cell, change Vert: to `Top` and Horz: to `Left`. While your cursor is in the lower right cell, enter the following text:

```
Don't see your question here? Please send your query to
faq@hotcooltoys.com for a response within 24 hours. When you
are submitting your question, please be sure to mention the
product in your question, or we will not be able to respond.
```

14. Select the text that reads:

```
faq@hotcooltoys.com
```

Press Ctrl+C (Command+C) to copy the text to the clipboard and using the Property inspector, type **mailto:** in the Link: field. Press Ctrl+V (Command+V) to paste the clipboard contents to make the link appear as follows:

```
mailto:faq@hotcooltoys.com
```

Press the Tab key to make the changes.

15. In the top left cell, you want the specific image to be displayed depending on the value of the `faqName` parameter. This is another location where you will use a `multipleif` conditional statement. Using Code view, type the following code the current cell (which should be the top left cell) or copy and paste from the file named `codefrag2.txt` in the site's `Local` folder. (If you use the latter method, be sure to paste in Code view, not Design view.)

```
<!-- TemplateBeginMultipleIf -->
    <!-- TemplateBeginIfClause cond="faqName=='bear'" --><img
src="../images/products/bear_b.jpg" alt="Teddy Bear" width="72"
height="108"><!-- TemplateEndIfClause -->
    <!-- TemplateBeginIfClause cond="faqName=='jack'" --><img
src="../images/products/jack_b.jpg" alt="Jack in the Box"
width="72" height="108"><!-- TemplateEndIfClause -->
    <!-- TemplateBeginIfClause cond="faqName=='kazoo'" --><img
src="../images/products/kazoo_b.jpg" alt="Krazy Kazoo" width="108"
height="72"><!-- TemplateEndIfClause -->
    <!-- TemplateBeginIfClause cond="faqName=='slinky'" --><img
src="../images/products/slinky_b.jpg" alt="Slippery Slinky"
width="108" height="72"><!-- TemplateEndIfClause -->
    <!-- TemplateBeginIfClause cond="faqName=='top'" --><img
src="../images/products/top_b.jpg" alt="Spinning Top" width="72"
height="108"><!-- TemplateEndIfClause -->
    <!-- TemplateBeginIfClause cond="faqName!='top'" --><span
class="error">Error - Error<br>faqName parameter must be one of
these: home, bear, jack, kazoo, slinky, or top!</span><!--
TemplateEndIfClause -->
<!-- TemplateEndMultipleIf -->
```

What you've done is set a specific image to display depending on the value of `faqName`, which is editable by the content editor. For instance, if you are on the "jack in the box" page, you would want the Jack in the Box image to display. You've also added some error checking to this `multipleif` so that if an allowed value for `faqName` is not set, the error message displays, advising the content editor of the allowed values.

16. Reposition your cursor (using Design view) in the top right cell. Insert a new table as outlined in Table 8.4.

Table 8.4   Inner FAQ Table

Field	Entry
Rows:	1
Cell Padding:	5
Columns:	2
Cell Spacing:	0
Width:	100 Percent
Border:	0

17. In the left cell of this new table, type a **"Q:"**. In the right cell of this table, type **"This product does not yet have any FAQs."** Select both cells of this new table and make it a repeating region using Insert > Template Objects > Repeating Region. In the dialog that is displayed, change the Name: field to **"RepFAQ"** and click OK.

18. Select the text `This product does not yet have any FAQs` in the right cell and insert an editable region named `FAQContent` using Insert > Template Objects > Editable Region.

19. Position your cursor in the left cell of this repeating table, and type **Q & A**. Select the contents of the cell, or by using the Tag Selector, click the `<TD>` and press Ctrl+B (Command+B) to bold the selection.

20. Close the page, saving changes and updating pages if prompted.

21. Let's create the child pages now. Select File > New, select the Templates tab and select the newly created template named `HCTNestedFAQs.dwt`. Make sure that there is a check in the Update Page when Template Changes field and click the Create button to close the dialog and create the new page.

22. Immediately save the file as `faqs.htm` in the site root. You didn't change the value of the parameter named `faqName` in the Template Properties because its default value in the template is `home`, which is where you want to be.

23. Now, as outlined in Table 8.5, change each parameter value and use File > Save As save the page.

Table 8.5   Parameter/Page Name Values

FaqName Value	Filename
bear	faqs_bear.htm
jack	faqs_jack.htm
kazoo	faqs_kazoo.htm
slinky	faqs_slinky.htm
top	faqs_top.htm

24. Using the instructions for adding content to the repeating region of the child page in the section, "Enhancing the Products Page," add your FAQs to the child pages you just created for the `faq` section of the site. The FAQ information can be used from the content created in Chapter 7.

    You may notice that for all the `faq` related pages you created, both optional regions are visible. This is not what you want at all. On the page with the `faqName` set to home (`faqs.htm`), you want only the `OptionBase` optional region to be shown and `OptionFAQTable` to be hidden. On all other `faq` pages, you want the reverse to be true.

25. Open `faqs_bear.htm`.

26. Select Modify > Template Properties. In the dialog that opens, select `OptionBase` and remove the check from the Show OptionBase checkbox and click OK.

After the dialog closes, the optional region `OptionBase` should disappear from the page.

Repeat this step for each FAQ page, excluding `faqs.htm` that would require you to select `OptionFAQTable`. Remove the check from Show OptionFAQTable. Don't do anything else to the pages; you will be automating the process later in this chapter in the section, "Automating the FAQ Optional Regions"

27. Save the page and close it. The completed template appears in Figure 8.2.

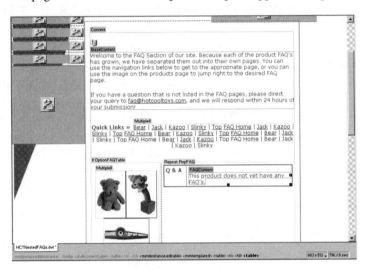

Figure 8.2   The finished nested FAQ template.

Modifications to the Nested Templates

You can do so many things to change the way these templates function and automate processes that it can be confusing to consider them all. For purposes of this text, we have chosen to explain two specific examples. This section gives you instructions for alternating table row coloring of the products page, and for automating the insertion of the Q and A on the product-specific FAQ pages.

Alternating Table Row Colors in Products.htm

Instead of having all the products display in the list with a white background, you may want to alternate table row colors. You can use individual cell Bg: coloring to achieve this, but that means that you have to do quite a bit by hand. Instead, let's do it programmatically so that the template engine does the work for us in the repeating table.

Exercise 8.4:   Modifying the Product's Nested Template to Output Alternating Row Colors

This exercise explains how to use a template expression to make a repeating table automatically change table row colors.

1. Open the template named HCTNestedProducts.dwt.

2. In the second row of the Products table, select the three white background cells (row 2, columns 2 through 4).

3. Change the Bg: value in the Property inspector from #FFFFFF to @@(_index%2 ? '#D0D0D0' : '#E4E4E4')@@ and press Tab to activate the changes.

4. Save the changes to the template and update the pages when prompted.

5. Open products.htm and preview it. Notice that the rows do have alternating colors (see Figure 8.3).

6. Close all open documents.

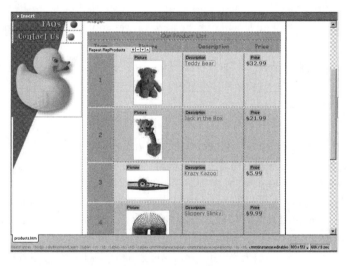

Figure 8.3   A child page of the nested products template.

> **Note**
>
> The background of these three cells changes back to orange from white because the template does not evaluate the expression to calculate the proper color of the cells. To view the proper colors, save the changes to the template and open its child page.

Sure, the table doesn't look great with the white background colors...but you get the idea of what's happening here. The expression was well-covered in Chapter 3, so you can turn to that chapter if you want to review how that expression works. The only differ-ence between the explanation in Chapter 3 and this section is that in Chapter 3 the expression is being applied to the `<tr>` tag, and this example applies it to three table cells, like this:

```
<td bgcolor="@@(_index%2 ? '#D0D0D0' : '#E4E4E4')@@">
```

You could easily apply this also to the FAQ table to give each Q row a different color than the A row by applying the same method to the `HCTNestedFAQs` repeating table.

Alternating Q and A in the FAQ repeating table

Instead of having Q and A on every row, or want only the Q or the A to display. You can do this by hand by making the region an editable region and having the content editor change it for each line in the child pages. This can lead to error, however, and it adds one more thing to the content editor's list of things to remember. Instead, let's take it out of the content editor's hands and do it programmatically so that the template engine does the work in the repeating table without the need for yet another editable region.

Exercise 8.5:   Modifying the FAQs Nested Template to Output Alternating Text Based on an Expression Value

This exercise explains how to make a repeating table automatically change a cell's con-tent, using a template expression.

 1. Open the template named `HCTNestedFAQ.dwt`.

 2. In the second row of the FAQ table, change `<strong>Q &amp; A</strong>` to

    `<strong>@@((_index % 2) ? "A:" : "Q:" )@@</strong>`

    This checks the value of the row. If the value is even, it inserts a bolded Q; if odd, it inserts a bolded A. That's one less thing that the content editor has to worry about changing in the child pages!

 3. Save the changes to the template and update the pages when prompted.

 4. Open `faqs_bear.htm` and preview it. Notice that the rows have indeed alternat-ing text of Q: and A: (see Figure 8.4).

 5. Close all open documents.

Figure 8.4   A child page of the nested faqs template.

Automating the FAQ Optional Regions

We have added three parameters to the nested template: `OptionBase`, `OptionFAQTable`, and `faqName`. This means that each child page needs to have three template properties configured each time a new page is created. What a hassle! We can fix it so that only one needs to be modified. If the others are changed, it has no effect at all on the parameters, thereby reducing a chance of error caused during content addition (just as you did for the base template).

Exercise 8.6:   Using an Expression to Control Optional Regions

Let's modify the template so that it is even more automated and less error-prone! Remember that you have two optional regions and one static area in the layer. Only one optional region will show on any given page, and the FAQ Home page needs to have introductory text, while the remaining FAQ sub-pages need to display the content table. This will behave like a toggle for the optional regions; when one is on, the other is off, and vice-versa.

1. Open the template named `HCTNestedFAQ.dwt`.

2. Using Code view, locate the code that reads:

   ```
   <!-- InstanceBeginEditable name="Content" --> <!-- TemplateBeginIf
   cond="OptionBase" -->
   ```

   Position your cursor at the front of the code that reads `<!-- TemplateBeginIf cond="OptionBase" -->` and insert the following expression:

```
<!-- @@(OptionFAQTable=!(OptionBase=(faqName=='home' ? true :
false)))@@ -->
```

The line should now look like this:

```
<!-- InstanceBeginEditable name="Content" -->
<!-- @@(OptionFAQTable=!(OptionBase=(faqName=='home' ?
true : false)))@@ --><!-- TemplateBeginIf cond="OptionBase" -->
```

This line will be represented in Design view as a standard HTML comment icon (if you have them turned on in Visual Aids).

You put comments around it to suppress the display of the expression, which generates a true or false result. All you want from this complex expression is to set the value of OptionFAQTable and OptionBase, based on the value of faqName.

But, what does this expression do? you ask. Let's break it down into more manageable chunks.

(OptionBase=(faqName=='home' ? true : false)) checks for the value of faqName as set through Template Properties menu item. If it is equal to home, OptionBase is set to true (Display); otherwise, it is set to false (Hide). By adding OptionFAQTable!= to the front of the expression, you are telling the expression to assign the inverse of OptionBase to OptionFAQTable. So if OptionBase is true, OptionFAQTable is false, thereby controlling the display value of both optional regions using one template expression.

3. Save the changes to the template and update the pages when prompted.

4. Open faqs_jack.htm and preview it. Notice that the OptionFAQTable area is showing and the OptionBase area is hidden. Go ahead and set OptionBase and OptionFAQTable to any value you like using Modify > Template Properties. The changes you make to these two parameters will have no effect on the page, which in turn reduces the chance of the content editor making a mistake or forgetting to set the parameters.

5. Open faqs.htm and preview it. The reverse of step 4 should be true. OptionBase should be showing and OptionFAQTable should be hidden—and we didn't have to touch a thing!

6. Close all open documents and finally, close Dreamweaver MX.

You've now learned what complex expressions can do! To recap, they can control which regions are displayed, they can control other parameters, and they can display certain images and hide others. Very powerful stuff!

Summary

This has been a pretty exhausting chapter in which you converted the site from a single template to one that partially uses nested templates (Products and FAQ pages). You've also explored the use of optional regions and used expressions to evaluate a value dependant on a table row index number to output either alternating colored rows or automating the insertion of a Q or A in a table row cell.

Take what you have learned from the entire book and practice on your own sites. Show us how you use complex templates and complex expressions in your sites by sending us an email to brag@dreamweavermx-templates.com detailing your problem, your solution, and the URL.

The finished templates and site you created in this chapter can be downloaded in the file Finished_8.zip from our support site, if you would like to compare your results with the actual end-product as designed. Murray and I will be around to assist where we can and have designed a web site specifically for the support of this book. Please visit us at our support site, located at www.dreamweavermx-templates.com.

Index

VOICES THAT MATTER

HOW TO CONTACT US

VISIT OUR WEB SITE

WWW.NEWRIDERS.COM

On our web site, you'll find information about our other books, authors, tables of contents, and book errata. You will also find information about book registration and how to purchase our books, both domestically and internationally.

EMAIL US

Contact us at: **nrfeedback@newriders.com**

- If you have comments or questions about this book
- To report errors that you have found in this book
- If you have a book proposal to submit or are interested in writing for New Riders
- If you are an expert in a computer topic or technology and are interested in being a technical editor who reviews manuscripts for technical accuracy

Contact us at: **nreducation@newriders.com**

- If you are an instructor from an educational institution who wants to preview New Riders books for classroom use. Email should include your name, title, school, department, address, phone number, office days/hours, text in use, and enrollment, along with your request for desk/examination copies and/or additional information.

Contact us at: **nrmedia@newriders.com**

- If you are a member of the media who is interested in reviewing copies of New Riders books. Send your name, mailing address, and email address, along with the name of the publication or web site you work for.

BULK PURCHASES/CORPORATE SALES

The publisher offers discounts on this book when ordered in quantity for bulk purchases and special sales. For sales within the U.S., please contact: Corporate and Government Sales (800) 382-3419 or **corpsales@pearsontechgroup.com**. Outside of the U.S., please contact: International Sales (317) 581-3793 or **international@pearsontechgroup.com**.

WRITE TO US

New Riders Publishing
201 W. 103rd St.
Indianapolis, IN 46290-1097

CALL/FAX US

Toll-free (800) 571-5840
If outside U.S. (317) 581-3500
Ask for New Riders
FAX: (317) 581-4663

New Riders

Publishing
the Voices
that Matter

OUR AUTHORS

PRESS ROOM

| web development | design | photoshop | new media | 3-D | server technologies |

EDUCATORS

ABOUT US

CONTACT US

You already know that New Riders brings you the **Voices That Matter**.

But what does that mean? It means that New Riders brings you the

Voices that challenge your assumptions, take your talents to the next

level, or simply help you better understand the complex technical world

we're all navigating.

Visit **www.newriders.com** to find:

- ▸ **10% discount** and **free shipping** on all book purchases
- ▸ Never before published chapters
- ▸ Sample chapters and excerpts
- ▸ Author bios and interviews
- ▸ Contests and enter-to-wins
- ▸ Up-to-date industry event information
- ▸ Book reviews
- ▸ Special offers from our friends and partners
- ▸ Info on how to join our User Group program
- ▸ Ways to have your Voice heard

New
Riders

WWW.NEWRIDERS.COM

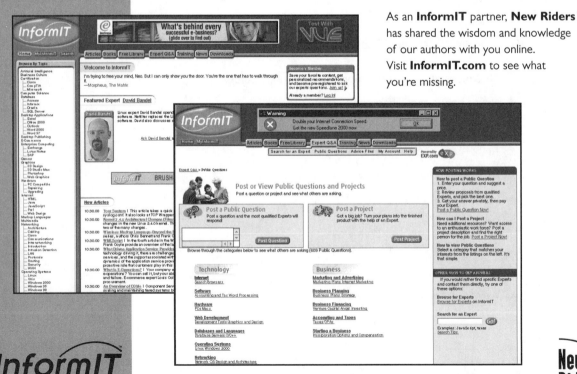

Colophon

As children, we all come to know and love the guided creativity of paint-by-number projects. The cover image was created in Photoshop by New Riders graphic designer, Aren Howell, with this innocence of creation in mind. Similarly, the template features of Dreamweaver MX give a web artist a blueprint for success.

This book was written and edited in Microsoft Word, and laid out in QuarkXPress. The font used for the body text is Bembo and Mono. It was printed on 50# Husky Offset Smooth paper at R.R. Donnelley & Sons in Crawfordsville, Indiana. Prepress consisted of PostScript computer-to-plate technology (filmless process). The cover was printed at Moore Langen Printing in Terre Haute, Indiana, on 12 pt., coated on one side.